Design Drawing Experiences

2000 Edition

William Kirby Lockard

W. W. Norton & Company
New York • London

Copyright © 2000, 1993, 1987, 1979, 1976, 1974, 1973 by
William Kirby Lockard

For information about permission to reproduce selections from this
book, write to Permissions, W. W. Norton & Company, Inc.,
500 Fifth Avenue, New York, NY 10110

The text and display of this book is composed in Sabon
Composition by Ken Gross
Manufacturing by Von Hoffmann Graphics, Inc. and Phoenix Color Corp.

Library of Congress Cataloging-in-Publication Data
Lockard, William Kirby, 1929–
 Design drawing experiences / William Kirby Lockard.—2000 ed.
  p. cm.
  ISBN 0-393-73041-7 (pbk.)
  1. Architectural Drawing. 2. Architectural rendering.

NA2705 .L622 2000
720'.28'4—dc21   99-086189

W.W. Norton & Company, Inc., 500 Fifth Avenue,
New York, NY 10110
www.wwnorton.com

W.W. Norton & Company Ltd., 10 Coptic Street,
London WC1A 1PU

3 4 5 6 7 8 9 0

I need to thank two people for their help in producing the 2000
edition of *Design Drawing* and *Design Drawing Experiences*:
Nancy Green, the editor at Norton, to whose interest in the
books, loyalty to the ideas, and insistence on quality this edition
owes its existence; and Casey Ruble, who not only tightened up
the writing and eliminated most of its redundancies, but who also
challenged me to clarify my ideas and explanations.

Contents

Preface

This 2000 edition of *Design Drawing Experiences* comes twenty-seven years after the first edition, which was copyrighted in 1973. Not many books on drawing have enjoyed so long a shelf life. Maybe *Design Drawing Experiences* has lasted because it is one of the only drawing books that includes actual exercises designed to help students learn the various drawing procedures and skills, and because I have revised those exercises and the instructions that go with them seven times in response to feedback from students in my own classes and in workshops at various schools around the country. The book has also benefited from new exercises I developed for the *Design Drawing Videotapes* I began recording in 1986.

Design Drawing Experiences is interdisciplinary and intended for students of architecture, landscape architecture, and interior design. It may be most unusual in that it has always assumed that drawing is essential for all environmental designers wanting to generate, manipulate, and communicate their design ideas; and, unlike most books on drawing, it is not for connoisseurs to collect, admire, and compare, but rather is intended to help its readers actually learn to draw.

I am proud that this book has continued for twenty-seven years to be a testament to the fact that drawing is a necessary skill for designers and that drawing, far from being the result of a genetic accident or providential gift, is one of the most learnable skills a designer needs.

The 2000 edition includes new exercises and drastic revisions of several old exercises. Throughout my years of teaching I have found that many students with strong drafting backgrounds understand the more technical procedures for laying out perspectives and casting shadows quite well. But when they are faced with adding materials, figures, furniture, and landscaping to their perspectives, they experience great frustration, lose the confidence they gained in perspective drawing, and thereafter avoid drawing perspectives.

With this in mind, I have reversed the order in which direct freehand perspective is presented. Now students first learn to add the finishing touches to their drawings. Later, when they have learned how to cast shadows in perspective and, finally, lay out the perspective itself, they will already have had enough practice in adding entourage that their drawings will be a source of pride and enjoyment.

I have also tried to point out that designers need two quite different ways of representing and studying their environmental designs: as objects that are to be built and as environments that are to be experienced. For the objective study of design, orthographic drawings are required, both during the design process and in producing the construction documents from which the object will be built. But the subjective experience of the design as an environment is dependent upon eyelevel perspectives. These should be drawn while the design process is still open to change and can be influenced by the environmental experience the perspectives provide.

While it includes a section on orthographic drawing, *Design Drawing Experiences* is primarily intended to help students draw freehand eyelevel perspectives, which are seldom made because architects are often content to conceive, study, and represent their buildings as if they were television sets or toasters, never to be entered or occupied, and viewed entirely from the outside.

This edition retains coordination with the *Design Drawing Videotapes* and I encourage the users of *Design Drawing Experiences* to explore the use of videos in teaching and learning drawing because the medium nicely supplements even the best book or live teacher.

I believe this is by far the best edition of *Design Drawing Experiences*, and I hope it will help you to learn to draw.

William Kirby Lockard, FAIA

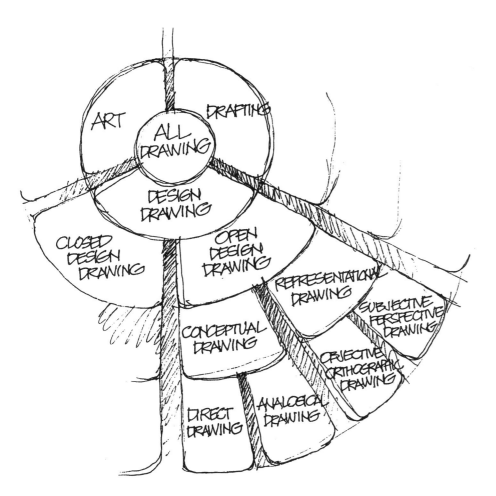

Introduction

For the 2000 edition, *Design Drawing Experiences* deserves a new introduction based on what I have learned using and revising the experiences in this book and thinking about the teaching and learning of what I began calling "design drawing" over a quarter of a century ago. I don't want to burden this exercise book with too many theories about drawing—that is the role of the companion text *Design Drawing*—but I would like to be clear and precise about the kind of drawing this book promotes and its relationship to other kinds of drawing and to the design process.

KINDS OF DRAWING. Basic to an understanding of the subject and purpose of this book is a clarification of the way I propose to parse drawing. The most basic separation of the various kinds of drawing is into drawing as art, drawing as drafting, and drawing as design drawing. Design drawing is quite different from the more conventional categories of art and drafting in that it serves an open decision-making process that produces the design of an environment.

The most basic distinction in design drawing is between drawing as an open-minded exploration and drawing as close-minded illustration. Open design drawing can be further divided into conceptual drawing and representational drawing. It is usually conceded that conceptual drawing is open-minded. Serious representational drawings, on the other hand, are often mistakenly assumed to be close-minded, persuasive "animations" used to sell the design rather than improve it. Perspective drawings are especially prone to this assumption.

Conceptual drawing, which includes both analogical and direct drawing, generates the first diagrammatic solutions for the design. Representational drawings are more literal interpretations of the design: orthographic drawings represent a design objectively as an object, and perspectives represent the subjective experience of the design as an environment.

You may be impatient with what may seem a compulsive categorization of the various kinds of drawing, preferring to continue conceiving of drawings in the familiar but irrelevant categories of media and form (pencil perspective, ink plan) that we inherit from art and drafting. But anyone who uses, and certainly anyone who teaches, drawing professionally should understand that the way we think about what we do has more influence on our behavior than anything else. We have been very sloppy in the way we describe and think about the various kinds of drawing used in the design professions; a certain rigor in the use of terms and a recognition of differences will help us all.

DRAWING TODAY AND TOMORROW. The increasing use of the computer for drawing is clarifying the way we think about the exercise. The computer is taking over the more repetitive, tedious drawing tasks, as I predicted it would in *Drawing as a Means to Architecture* (1968). We should be grateful for that change, because it leaves us free to do the other things we do best—like generating and evaluating design ideas—those things the computer cannot yet do, may never be able to do, and, perhaps, should never be allowed to do.

Computer drawing is also helping us to make decisions as to what kinds of skills are worth acquiring. Regrettably, some serious mistakes are being made. Some kinds of drawing skills may no longer be worth mastering—like drafting and lettering—because the computer can already do them more quickly and more accurately. Other skills are worth mastering even if the computer can do them. It may take hours to build a computer model of an environment a skilled designer can sketch in minutes. Drawings of landscaping, furniture, automobiles, and human figures still need to be drawn by hand if a perspective is to have any character or life. A layer of hand drawing over a computer-generated wire frame is still absolutely necessary to produce the best rendering.

FREEHAND PERSPECTIVES. Although *Design Drawing Experiences* has been revised and enlarged over the years to include all the kinds of design drawings, its emphasis remains on open, subjective, freehand perspective drawings that include shadows and entourage and present the design as an environment to be experienced. Designers must be able to draw quick freehand eyelevel perspectives not only for their clients but also for themselves, just as composers play their musical compositions for themselves or as poets scribble their poems and read them aloud to themselves. We also are discovering that this personal, conceptual end of the drawing spectrum is the area where the computer has the least to contribute.

VARIOUS DESIGNERS. The design drawing experiences are intended to be appropriate for students of architecture, landscape architecture, and interior design. The variety of experiences will allow students in introductory multidisciplinary courses to consider which of these various design disciplines most interests them.

USING THE BOOK. My experience in teaching drawing is that the development and grading of drawing exercises is a very time-consuming, potentially boring task. Yet interesting, carefully corrected exercises are basic to any teaching or learning of drawing. This is particularly important for today's young people, who may have had very little repetitive practice in their education. With drill and memorization so disdained by many of today's educators, young people not involved in athletics, music, dance, or drama may see little value in iterative experience. These students may do a handskills exercise once and, no matter how poorly it was executed, see little value in doing it again.

Consequently, drawing tasks must interest, challenge, or tease students into making a succession of drawings they can recognize as being successful and worth the effort. Exercises should also leave room for students' personal creativity. Design drawing exercises should ask for and value students' contributions, not just ask them to be copying machines. The purpose of teaching drawing should be entirely to turn a student on to drawing.

While drawing tasks should be interesting and value design creativity, they should never be permissive. The basic skills to be learned in design drawing are perhaps comparable to those of English grammar and spelling. The skills allow you to be eloquent, but the fundamentals must be mastered first and the teacher must insist that there is a mandatory discipline to drawing a line, casting a shadow, or structuring a perspective.

EXPERIENCES. Although drawing is certainly physical and requires great hand-eye coordination, I object to the exclusive use

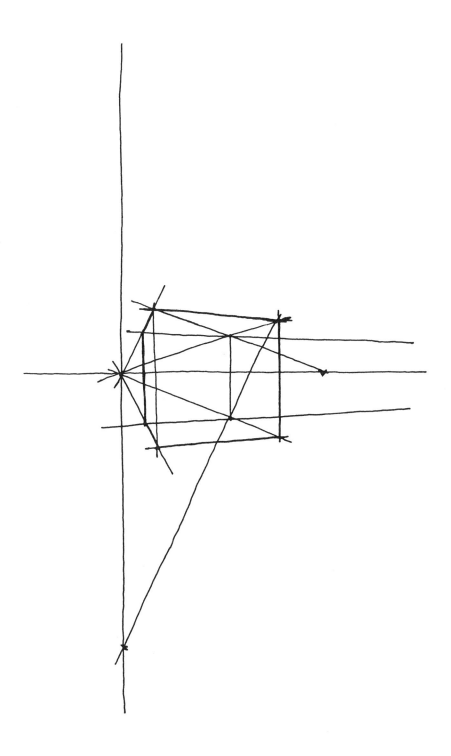

of the word *exercise* to describe the assigned tasks intended to help a student learn to draw. Most drawing mistakes are head mistakes, not hand mistakes; they are mistakes of judgment rather than of hand-eye coordination. There is a great deal about drawing that must be understood intellectually—if you were to insist on locating drawing ability physically, I would argue that it exists somewhere above the shoulder, not below.

Exercise suggests calisthenics, which excludes thinking or cognitive learning and promotes the Cartesian legacy of mind/body separation. *Experiences* communicates an involvement of body, mind, and even the emotions in the simple pleasure of making a beautiful drawing.

The design drawing experiences collected in this book should help students develop their drawing skills and experience the relationship between what is being drawn and what is being designed. This is further described in the accompanying text, *Design Drawing*. The experiences in this book are intended to be assigned in class but should be supported by the theory and instruction in *Design Drawing*.

USING THE EXERCISES. I usually assign each exercise in this book to be completed in a single three-hour studio, after a draw-along session that goes over the new procedures or skills required. I call these "pressure drawings" and I post all of them in the corridor at the end of the studio so students can compare their progress to others in the class. By the sixth or seventh week we are laying out simple perspectives, casting shadows, adding entourage, and coloring the drawings in a single studio.

This kind of drawing under pressure is complemented by six-week homework assignments on which the students spend as much time as possible. These two ways of drawing—quickly, under the pressure of a very short and inflexible time period, and slowly, over a much longer period—provide a valuable contrast and balance in learning to draw and require two different kinds of self-management skills.

The experiences are intended to be interesting and rewarding, allowing students to experience the pleasure of making a drawing they recognize as successful and helping them to understand exactly how the success was accomplished. Instead of being a test of success versus failure, they should inspire students and teach them success and confidence.

At the beginning of each set of experiences is a brief explanation of its purpose and the skills or procedures required. Instructors may choose to change the assignment or criteria according to their own ways of drawing or teaching drawing. Students will soon realize that there are many ways to draw, and the responsibility of the teacher is to teach the way she or he thinks is true or best, demanding that students try that way, but ultimately to encourage them to develop their own ways of drawing.

Students can work directly on the sheets provided or overlay them with an 8½"-by-11" sheet of tracing paper and vary them according to additional instructions. Some of the exercises are printed on tracing paper so that after they are completed they can be blueprinted and then colored; this will help students gain experience in using reproduction techniques. Most of the experiences can be supplemented by changing the light assumption or by asking for the delineation of furniture, materials, people, or plants. Many of the frameworks are multipurpose and can be used for various combinations of drawing experiences; they can also be enlarged to make 11" x 17" or larger renderings. The duplicate frameworks on gray paper are for assignments using black-and-white-on-middletone drawing techniques.

Because most students coming to architectural education have had experience in pencil drafting, I insist that they draw freehand, with a pen, for several reasons. First, I want them to get in the habit of overlaying their rough layout drawings so that they visualize any drawing task as potentially a stack of overlaid drawings that progress from very rough layout drawings on the bottom to very finished drawings on the top. Instead of erasing and redrawing, they simply overlay and improve, discounting the value of any particular drawing over another and emphasizing the process of improving a drawing.

Second, I insist that they draw freehand so that they become confident without the crutch of a straightedge. I tell them that the pursuit of the perfect drafted orthographic drawing has been lost to the computer and is no longer worth human effort, that they'll never be able to draft trees, cars, and figures with a straightedge, and that the only fit companion to a free mind is a free hand.

Additionally, drawing freehand with ink takes away the advantage of their pencil drafting experience and teaches them an alternative way of drawing. This helps them to get used to the idea of developing other ways of drawing, eventually allowing them the freedom to make deliberate choices in drawing rather than relying on the only way they know.

One last note: I favor drawing on buff tracing paper for several reasons. First, it is the most inexpensive, fragile medium available, which helps to prevent any single drawing from becoming overly important. Second the use of white and other light Prismacolor™ pencils on tracing paper is a highly effective way of depicting light and shadows. Third, the transparency of the paper promotes the use of successive overlays and allows for the application of colors and tones on the back of the paper, which softens and improves the appearance of the drawing and doesn't conflict with the ink lines on the front.

I wish you well in learning to draw. Drawing ability should not be based on a collection of mysterious techniques that those in the design professions keep secret from one another. We will all benefit if we learn to draw better and share the knowledge as broadly as possible.

1 Conceptual Drawing

This chapter is concerned with drawing's relationship to the design process. Conceptual drawing is an interactive process that involves all the tools of human intelligence: eye, mind, and hand. It is not the neutral "printing out" of a previous, separate conceptual process.

Drawing is just as legitimate and useful a tool for thinking and problem-solving as language or mathematics; it just happens to be neglected in conventional education. We spend decades teaching our young people to use language and mathematics as tools of thought but spend little or no time teaching them to think with drawings, even in professional design schools.

Two of the best ways of using drawing conceptually are encouraged by the exercises that follow. The first is in drawing analogies for the problem you are trying to solve or for its solutions. Seeing how a problem or solution is like something you already know has proven to be one of the most creative problem-solving techniques.

The second use is in drawing conceptual diagrams that directly represent trial solutions to the problem. These direct drawings are usually plans or sections and may be translations from verbal statements or preverbal concepts whose verbal explanation actually comes after the drawing.

You should develop the habit of looking for design opportunities as you draw. As you become familiar with patterns and forms from historical or contemporary designs (Frank Ching's *Architecture: Form, Space, and Order* is an excellent collection) you will recognize the potential for various ordering systems in your conceptual drawings. You may see that with a few changes you can develop a strongly linear plan arrangement facing a view or generate a concentric arrangement of smaller spaces around a larger central space (see page 14). Looking for these opportunities to improve the design in your conceptual drawings allows you to use a very old and uniquely human ability—pattern recognition. Just as you can pick a familiar face out of thousands, if you show yourself a profusion of conceptual drawings you will be able to recognize opportunities that you would never discover with words or numbers. You must not stop thinking when you start drawing. It should be just the reverse—your design thinking should start when you begin to draw.

Clients verbalize their needs and aspirations for design projects. Your job will be to translate those verbal statements first into two-dimensional drawings and then into three-dimensional reality. Conceptual drawings like those required in the exercises that follow are the best way to begin to become fluent in the translation from verbal concepts to a well-designed environment.

ANALOGICAL DRAWING

This set of experiences is designed to help you develop the ability to use graphic analogies. One of the most valuable creative habits is discovering relationships between apparently unrelated ideas, especially when they appear to be opposites. The ability to recognize how a problem, a context, or a functional pattern is like something else we already know allows us to use our knowledge and past experience in solving problems.

A good analogy consists of two things that, beyond having obviously similar qualities, are often unexpectedly related in secondary levels of detail. For instance, it might occur to us that the design for a maximum-security entry is analogous to the security involved in protecting our stomachs from undesirable ingestion. It is immediately apparent that we can close our mouths and throats and clench our teeth. But as we continue to consider the analogy, and especially if we draw a section through it, we realize that whatever enters our mouth must tentatively be looked over by our eyes, be invited by our hand, and smelled as it passes under our nose. We further realize that there is also an extra inner door, the epiglottis, that protects the lungs, and if all else fails there is a gag reflex. The entry/mouth analogy is unexpectedly rich in the variety of security measures it suggests.

Drawing analogies is the best way to provoke a deeper understanding of them and their appropriateness for a particular problem or solution. Strong analogies are also one of the most effective ways of communicating design ideas to clients.

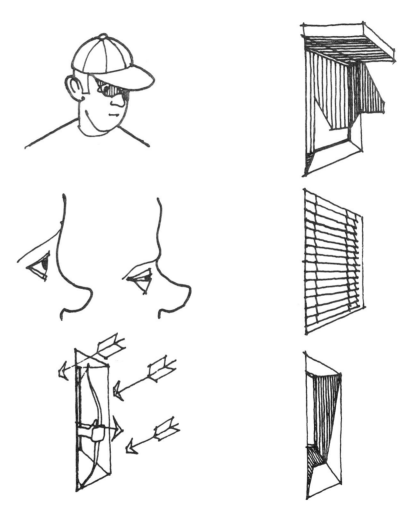

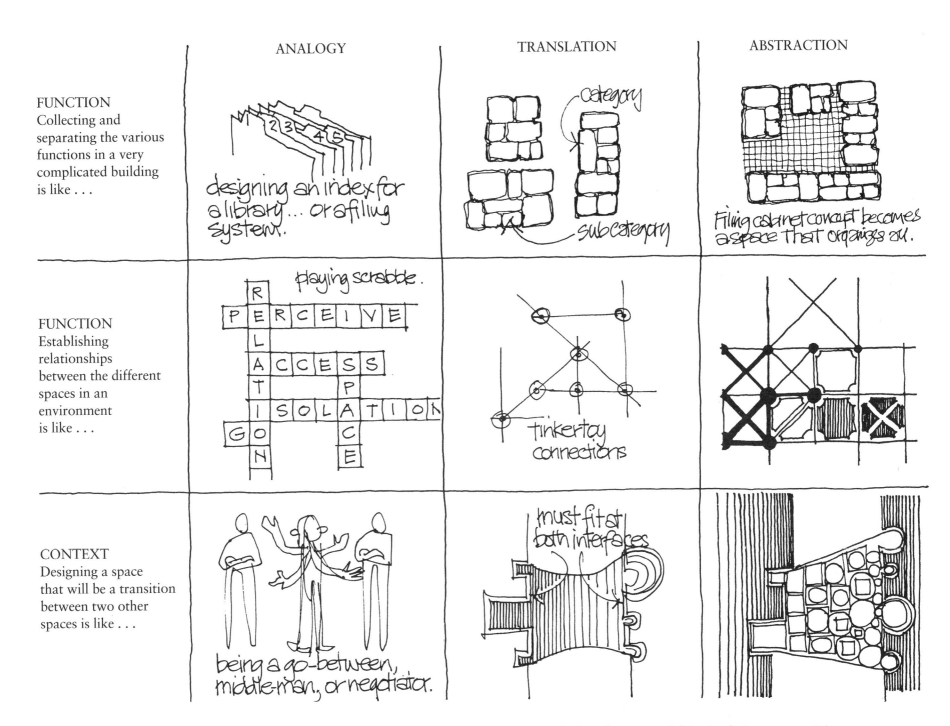

	ANALOGY	TRANSLATION	ABSTRACTION
FUNCTION Collecting and separating the various functions in a very complicated building is like . . .	designing an index for a library . . . or a filing system.	category ↓ subcategory	Filing cabinet concept becomes a space that organizes all.
FUNCTION Establishing relationships between the different spaces in an environment is like . . .	playing scrabble. R E L A T I O N / P E R C E I V E / A C C E S S / I S O L A T I O N / G O / S P A C E	tinkertoy connections	
CONTEXT Designing a space that will be a transition between two other spaces is like . . .	being a go-between, middle-man, or negotiator.	must fit at both interfaces	

EXPLANATION The above analogies and their translations into abstract diagrams are examples of the analogical drawings asked for in the following exercises. Most analogies must be translated into abstract diagrams before they are useful in the design process. Diagrams are often seen in final environmental designs, though at times they may serve only as catalysts and be replaced by better ideas.

11

FUNCTION	ANALOGY	TRANSLATION	ABSTRACTION
An environment with a functional requirement that it be easily maintained is like . . .			
A functional pattern that must happen in a particular linear order is like . . .			
A functional pattern involving the meeting and conversation of small groups of individuals is like . . .			

INSTRUCTIONS Conceive and draw analogies for the problems described above. Translate the analogies into graphic abstractions that capture the essence of the analogy in a memorable pattern, and refine these diagrams to their strongest forms. Some excellent analogies may not lead to clear graphic diagrams. The translation phase is nothing more than a rough attempt at a final abstraction. Feel free to include verbal explanatory notes, but try to let the graphic image tell the story.

CONTEXT	ANALOGY	TRANSLATION	ABSTRACTION
A building site surrounded by older buildings of great value is like . . .			
Preserving the exterior of a building while gutting and redesigning the interior is like . . .			
Designing a building to be built in a mature forest is like . . .			

INSTRUCTIONS Conceive and draw analogies for the problems described above. Translate the analogies into graphic abstractions that capture the essence of the analogy in a memorable pattern, and refine these diagrams to their strongest forms. Some excellent analogies may not lead to clear graphic diagrams. The translation phase is nothing more than a rough attempt at a final abstraction. Feel free to include verbal explanatory notes, but try to let the graphic image tell the story.

DIRECT DRAWING

These experiences are designed to help students recognize potential patterns and relationships, to manipulate them to their best form, and to communicate them graphically. Unlike analogical drawing, direct drawing is an attempt at graphic expression, and the analogy—the similarity to other problems or solutions—is only implied. The diagrams may represent the context, the functional pattern, or the proposed form in the plan or section of the problem to be solved.

Most formal patterns, at least the more sophisticated ones, are not obvious, especially to beginning designers. As in making analogies, we recognize potential patterns in our designs because we see how they are similar to (or can be made similar to) other familiar patterns. This is why good designers usually have an extensive knowledge of historical and contemporary examples of successful designs in their respective fields. They are quick to recognize potential relationships between the pattern in a problem's functional diagram or context and the patterns they remember from their own knowledge and experience.

The ability to design a context depends on some knowledge of what makes up all contexts—sun, wind, vegetation, surrounding buildings, views, pedestrian and automobile traffic—and of how these constituents may be related and expressed graphically.

A functional pattern in which many small spaces need to have a convenient relationship to a common large space could suggest the pattern in the upper right diagram. This abstract concept needs to be translated into a more buildable rectangular form (lower left) and then back, a little more abstractly, to the diagram at lower right, which shows landscaped spaces at the corners and a better entry.

The value in drawing the various aspects of design problems in diagrammatic form is that our minds can see, comprehend, and respond to more visual information than we can ever remember from verbal notes.

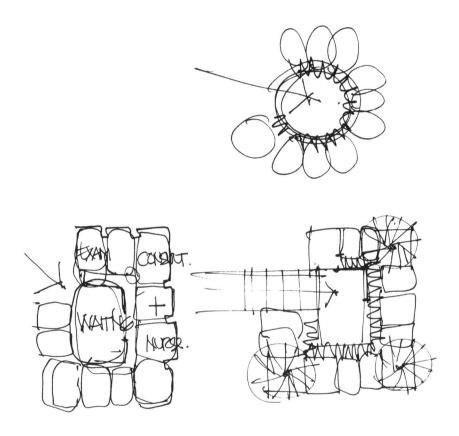

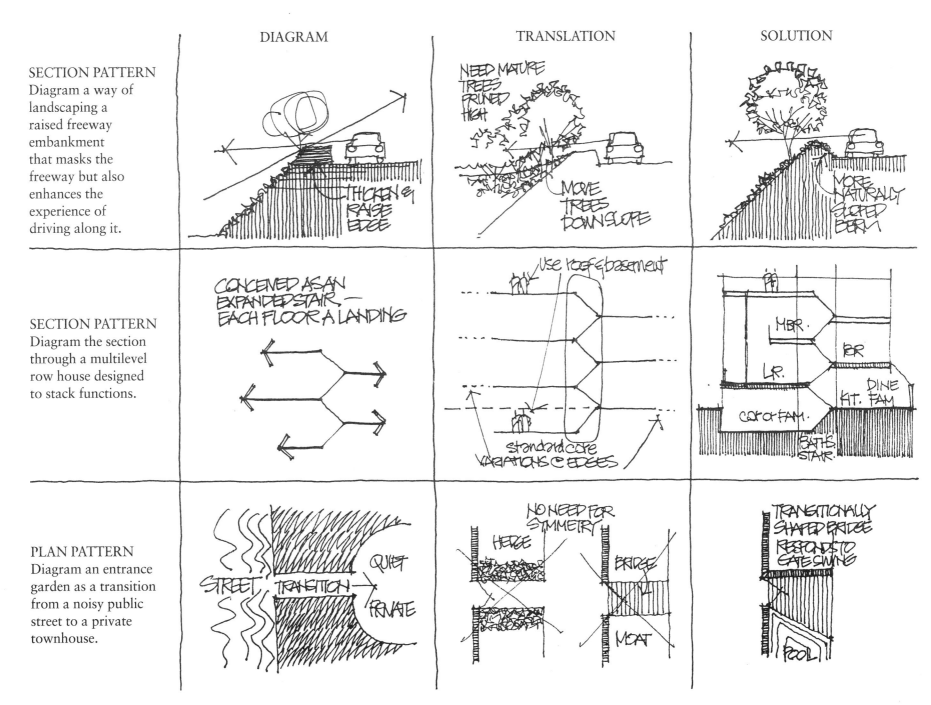

	DIAGRAM	TRANSLATION	SOLUTION
SECTION PATTERN Diagram a way of landscaping a raised freeway embankment that masks the freeway but also enhances the experience of driving along it.	THICKEN & RAISE EDGE	NEED MATURE TREES PRUNED HIGH / MOVE TREES DOWN SLOPE	MORE NATURALLY SLOPED BERM
SECTION PATTERN Diagram the section through a multilevel row house designed to stack functions.	CONCEIVED AS AN EXPANDED STAIR— EACH FLOOR A LANDING	Use roof & basement / standard core VARIATIONS @ EDGES	MBR. / LR. / BR / KT. FAM / DINE FAM / car & fam. / BATHS STAIR.
PLAN PATTERN Diagram an entrance garden as a transition from a noisy public street to a private townhouse.	STREET TRANSITION QUIET PRIVATE	NO NEED FOR SYMMETRY / HEDGE / BRIDGE / MOAT	TRANSITIONALLY SHAPED BRIDGE RESPONDS TO GATE SWING / POOL

EXPLANATION The diagrams above and their translation into designed environments are examples of the kind of direct drawing asked for in the succeeding exercises. The successful translation of diagrammatic concepts into built form depends on a broad and confident vocabulary of formal and material alternatives.

15

FUNCTION	DIAGRAM	TRANSLATION	SOLUTION
Diagram a cluster of diverse functions that share a common entry point.			
Diagram an exterior space that unifies two very different buildings.			
Diagram a circulation pattern through a museum that could be followed in one continuous sequence but allows shortcuts for selective museum-goers.			

INSTRUCTIONS Conceive and draw diagrams that directly express the relationships described above. Translate and refine the initial abstract diagrams into designed environments so that the essence and clarity of the original diagram are retained in the designed environment. Most of the diagrammatic patterns can be either plan patterns or section patterns.

16

PLAN PATTERNS	DIAGRAM	TRANSLATION	SOLUTION
Diagram a three-bedroom house in which the principal rooms all face the same view.			
Diagram a three-bedroom house arranged around an open courtyard.			
Diagram a three-bedroom house arranged around an indoor space like a living room or a family room.			

INSTRUCTIONS Conceive and draw diagrams that directly express the relationships described above. Translate and refine the initial abstract diagrams into designed environments in such a way that the essence and clarity of the original diagram are retained in the designed environment.

SECTION PATTERNS	DIAGRAM	TRANSLATION	SOLUTION
Diagram the section of a three-bedroom house that steps down a steep slope.			
Diagram the section of a two-story house that clusters around a two-story living room.			
Diagram a two-story house that strongly separates sleeping from waking activities.			

INSTRUCTIONS Conceive and draw diagrams that directly express the relationships described above. Translate and refine the initial abstract diagrams into designed environments in such a way that the essence and clarity of the original diagram are retained in the designed environment.

THE NEXT STEP:
REPRESENTATIONAL DRAWING

After direct conceptual drawings have established a concept, drawing can be used to represent the ideas so that they can be manipulated and refined. These representational drawings are very important because they represent the design to our eye-minds, and we must be careful to understand their strengths and weaknesses and the prejudices they carry. Of all dogma in design education, the conventional drawings and the order in which they are undertaken are the most strongly defended—if, indeed, they are ever questioned at all.

It is time we inquired critically into traditional representational drawings and their relationship to experience and to the design process, as well as into alternative techniques for making them. The ways of thinking about these drawings and the methods for making them advocated here are not proposed as the most technically accurate or artistically admired. However, I have found they can be understood and applied by design students with little previous drawing background. They work. My aim is to help students of design learn to use drawing as a design tool, not to teach students who already know how to draw to make masterpiece renderings.

The most important distinction within representative drawing is between orthographic drawings, which are made to study the design as an object to be constructed, and perspective drawings, which consider the design as an environment to be experienced.

②Orthographic (Objective) Drawing

Orthographic drawings (plans, sections, and paraline drawings) can completely, unequivocally describe a building, a landscape, or an interior and are indispensable in designing, estimating, and constructing an environment. Plans, sections, and elevations show each surface in a precise, measurable way that allows them to be efficiently drafted or programmed into one of the computer-aided drafting programs. Paraline drawings can depict designs three-dimensionally without giving up direct measurability.

Although more and more of our orthographic drawings will be made on the computer, designers still need to be able to draw plans, sections, and elevations by hand in order to conceive their designs. Quick, sketchy plans and sections are essential in conceiving and refining initial spatial concepts, and elevations are necessary to study fenestration and proportions. Although designers will develop their own way of transitioning to the computer, they need an understanding and mastery of orthographic drawings.

The traditional esthetics of well-drawn orthographic drawings are also necessary to make your computer drawings read correctly or have any character. The correct applications of line weights, background tones, and sheet composition are not automatic computer functions. For all these reasons designers will, in the foreseeable future, continue to learn to make orthographic drawings.

REPRESENTING A DESIGN AS AN OBJECT TO BE CONSTRUCTED

Orthographic drawings are called objective for several reasons. The strongest reason is that they represent whatever is being designed as an object, separated from the viewer spatially and further separated by being a view that is impossible to perceive in reality. Such objectivity is thought to promote the unbiased, unemotional neutrality much valued in scientific and judicial matters. Phrases in our language like "becoming emotionally involved," "taking it personally," and "losing your objectivity" all exalt the kind of detachment or even disinterest associated with scientific neutrality and unprejudiced judgment.

Certainly there is a need to study design in plan and section, and, less critically, in elevation, and also, if you've never learned to draw perspectives, in paraline drawings. This is especially true for architects studying the systems of a building they are designing. The structural plans must be logical and coordinated with the heating, air-conditioning, and electrical plans. In a ceiling there must be a coordination between lights and diffusers, and ducts must have adequate clearance under beams. These relationships only show in plans and sections.

Beyond these practical reasons for studying designs objectively in the orthographic drawings, there are also strong esthetic reasons for representing the design as an object. Well-designed objects or environments must have a certain integrity, an internal consistency or unity. Such a logical synthesis demands strong relationships between the design's constituent elements. The parts must make a satisfying whole, which is best studied in orthographic drawings.

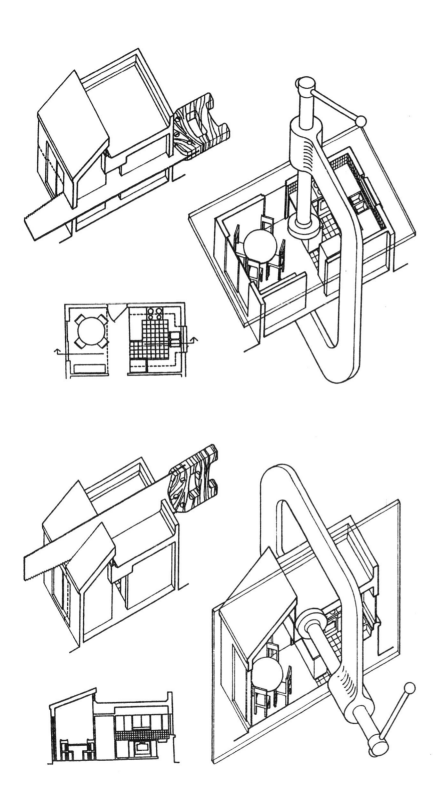

PLANS AND SECTIONS

Both plans and sections are sectional views that show what would be seen if you cut through a building or environment and removed the part above or in front of the slice. The plan is a view straight down at the floor of a building that has been cut horizontally in two and had the top half removed. The section is a side view of a building that has been cut vertically in two and had the front half removed. Plans and sections are most useful when used in a group of related views to describe a building or environment, with each drawing or view contributing to the understanding of the environment being described.

Plan and section drawings are abstractions because the lines and planes perpendicular to the plane of the slice do not converge toward a single central vanishing point (as they would in reality) but rather are perpendicular to the axis of our vision. Perhaps a simpler way of understanding this is to imagine that after the top or front of a building is cut away, we put the remaining building in a giant press and compress it into a thin wafer. In a floor plan the walls, kitchen counters, and furniture would be mashed flat into the floor and drawn as if they were simply a pattern in the linoleum. A section is similarly compressed into the back wall and any wall cabinets or furniture are drawn as if they were patterned wallpaper on that wall. The greatest advantage of this is that the surfaces or elements of a building that are parallel to the sectioning plane can be drawn without foreshortening or distortion of their true shape and size.

LINE WEIGHTS

The parts of the building that are compressed in a plan or section drawing are fundamentally different from one another and the drawing must tell what they were before the compression. This indication of difference is made by the kind of line representing them.

SPATIAL BOUNDARIES. The most important lines in plans or sections are the boundaries of the spaces that are cut through in removing the part of the building that allows the view. These lines indicate the boundaries of the volumes that make up the environment. The importance of this line is always indicated by making the line heavier or thicker than the other lines.

OBJECT OUTLINES. The second-most important lines, which are a slightly lighter weight than the spatial-boundary lines, are those that indicate the outline of objects within the space of a plan or section. These include attached counters, platforms or steps, and detached articles of furniture.

OBJECT DETAILS. Next in importance and line weight are the lines showing the details of an object. This kind of line indicates the burners on a stove, the depressed bowl of a lavatory seen in plan, and the recessed panels of a door seen in elevation.

SURFACE LINES. The lightest lines are those that carry no spatial information and simply lie on the horizontal surfaces of a plan or on the vertical surfaces of a section. Tile joints or other surface textural indications like wood grain or carpet texture are indicated with surface lines.

HIDDEN-EDGE LINES and REMOVED-EDGE LINES. Hidden-edge lines are those that occur beneath or beyond the plane featured in the plan or section. These hidden-edge lines show elements of construction and are rarely used in design drawings. Removed-edge lines are those that occur in the part of the building that was removed to draw the plan or section and of these, conventionally, only those in the plan are drawn. The critical removed-edge lines are those indicating the lines of overhanging planes, like roofs, balconies, and upper cabinets. Both hidden-edge lines and removed-edge lines are dashed and of the same weight as lines not hidden or removed.

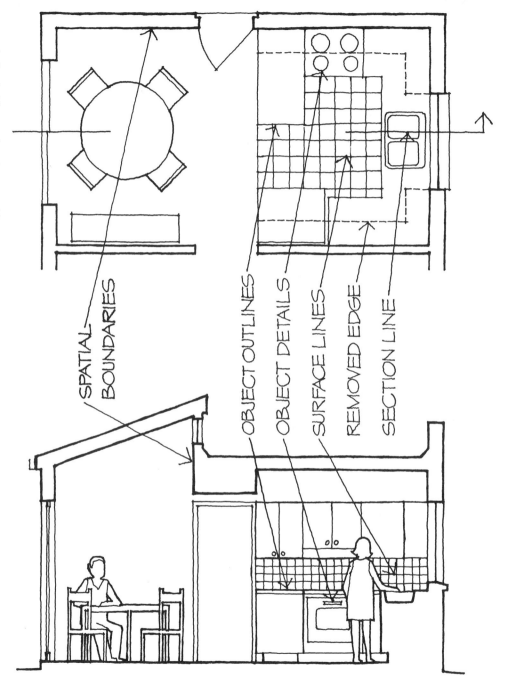

SPATIAL BOUNDARIES

OBJECT OUTLINES

OBJECT DETAILS

SURFACE LINES

REMOVED EDGE

SECTION LINE

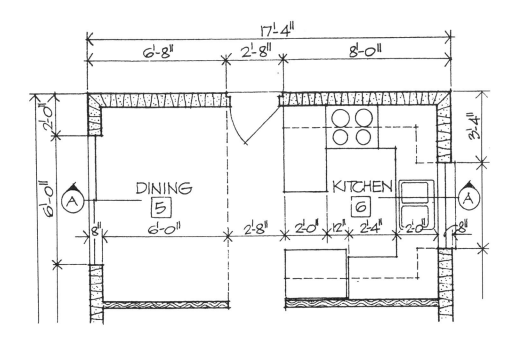

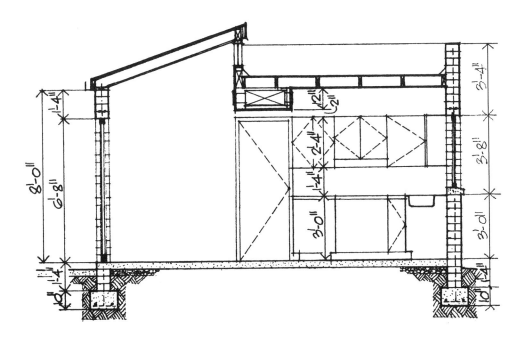

CUTTING PLANS AND SECTIONS

Floor plans should cut through the building at a height that goes through all wall openings, such as doors and windows. Generally, cutting through a building at a height of four feet above the floor will include most major vertical elements such as doors and windows, but this height can vary depending on what needs to be shown. Lines that occur above this section plane, such as dropped ceilings, roof overhangs, and skylights, should be indicated as dashed or dotted lines.

Care should be taken in choosing where to cut a section. A section should always be cut where it will show the greatest number of relationships between interior spaces and look toward the most significant ends of the various spaces. Sections should also be taken so that they show, in elevation, important elements of the building beyond where the section is cut. As with the plan, the section should also incorporate major elements, such as windows, doors, changes in roof and floor levels, roof openings, lofts, mezzanines, and fireplaces.

CONSTRUCTION DRAWINGS VERSUS DESIGN DRAWINGS

It is important to understand the difference between design drawings, like those on the previous page, and construction drawings, like those on this page—especially if you have experience in making construction drawings. The crucial difference between design drawings and construction drawings can be seen clearly by comparing the drawings' emphasis:

- Construction drawings describe the exact location, configuration, dimensions, and inner physical structure and consistency of the stuff of which the walls, the floor, and the roof are made.
- Design drawings describe the relative location, configuration, adequacy for human function, and the pattern of interrelationships of the spaces formed by the walls, the floor, and the roof.

The emphasis of construction drawings is on the solids, while the emphasis of design drawings is on the voids.

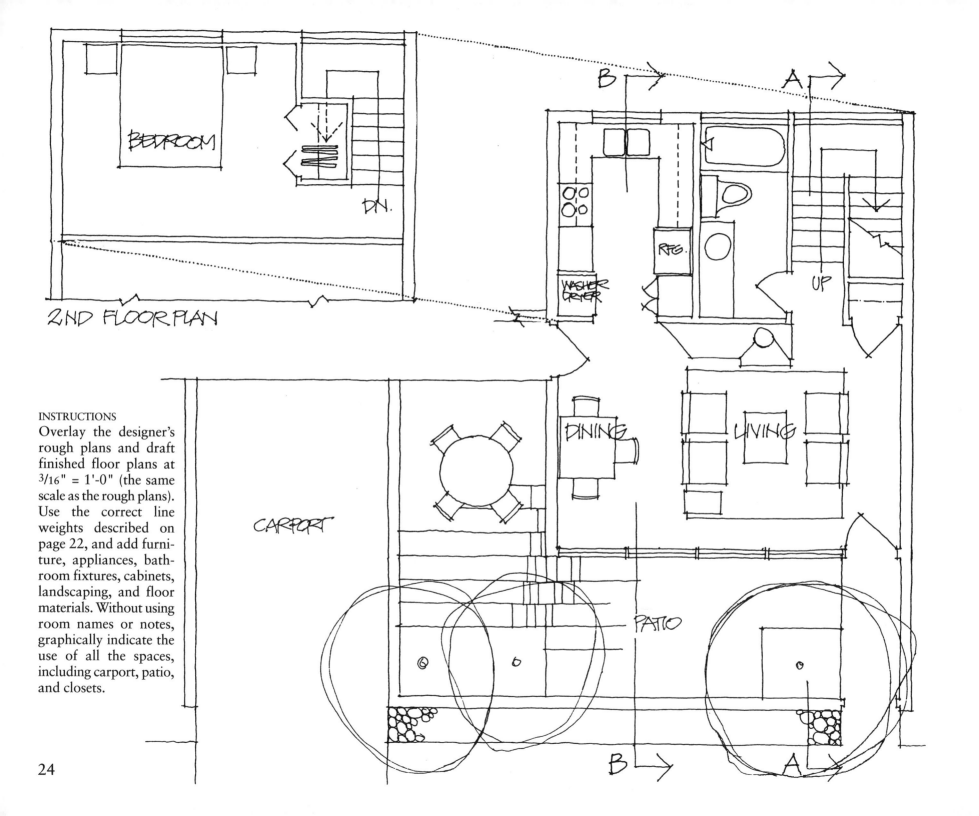

BEDROOM

DN.

2ND FLOOR PLAN

B

A

WASHER DRYER

RFG.

UP

INSTRUCTIONS
Overlay the designer's rough plans and draft finished floor plans at $3/16" = 1'-0"$ (the same scale as the rough plans). Use the correct line weights described on page 22, and add furniture, appliances, bathroom fixtures, cabinets, landscaping, and floor materials. Without using room names or notes, graphically indicate the use of all the spaces, including carport, patio, and closets.

CARPORT

DINING

LIVING

PATIO

B

A

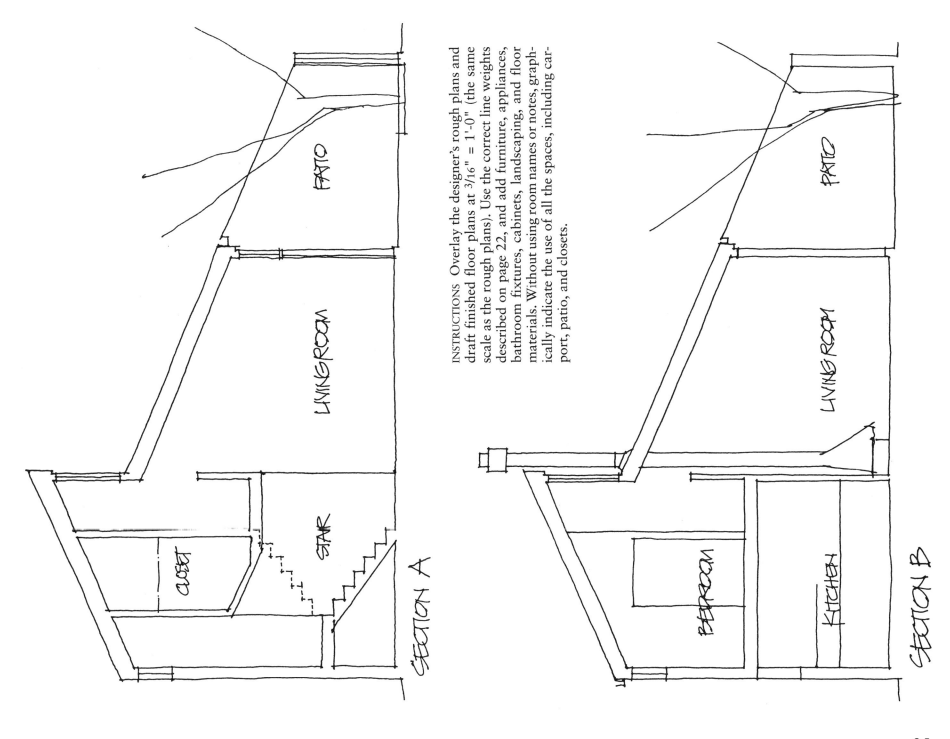

INSTRUCTIONS Overlay the designer's rough plans and draft finished floor plans at 3/16" = 1'-0" (the same scale as the rough plans). Use the correct line weights described on page 22, and add furniture, appliances, bathroom fixtures, cabinets, landscaping, and floor materials. Without using room names or notes, graphically indicate the use of all the spaces, including carport, patio, and closets.

PATIO

LIVING ROOM

CLOSET

STAIR

SECTION A

PATIO

LIVING ROOM

BEDROOM

KITCHEN

SECTION B

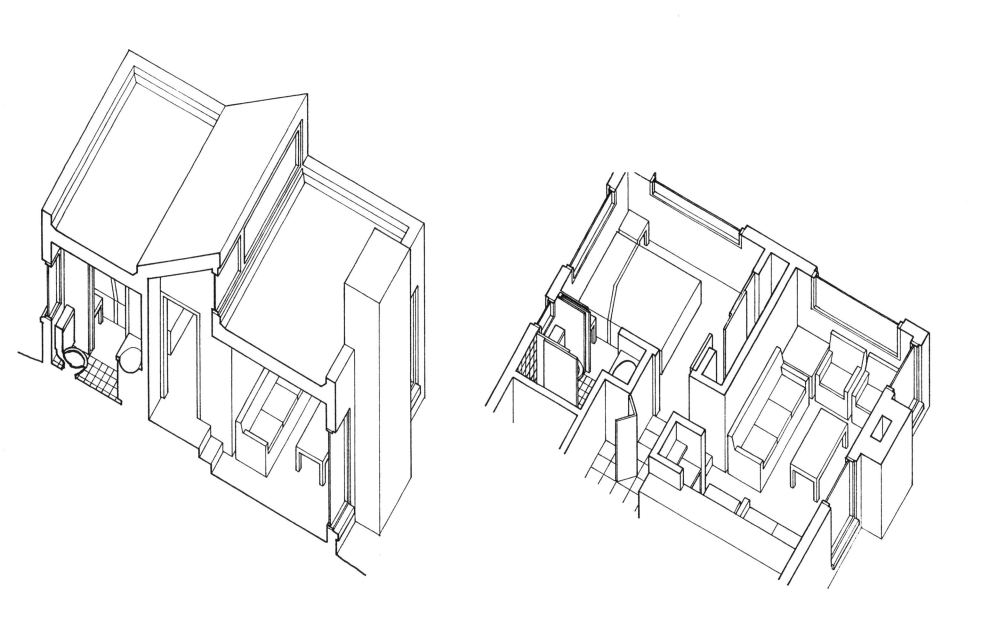

INSTRUCTIONS Draw a partial floor plan and a section from the information given in the two 3/16"-scale paraline drawings above. Choose an appropriate scale and use correct line weights to indicate a difference among the various types of lines.

PARALINE DRAWINGS

From the fragmented two-dimensional plans and sections, we progress in the hierarchy of realism to drawings closer to reality. These drawings show all three dimensions of an object at once. The most basic of them is called "axonometric" or "paraline." They are easily drawn, especially by drafting, making them a valuable part of a designer's vocabulary. Paraline drawings allow you to easily create a pictorial view more closely resembling natural perception than plans, sections, or elevations.

Because the paraline drawing is an aerial view, it is a good method to present the overall form or configuration of an object. Paraline drawings can also be used as either horizontal or vertical cutaways to provide a three-dimensional view of a building's interior. Construction details can convey more information, illustrate more relationships, and be more easily understood as paraline drawings.

While much easier to draw than perspectives, paraline drawings have some major drawbacks. Since parallel lines remain parallel and all orthogonal lines are directly measurable, the convergence and foreshortening of lines that we perceive in reality are lost. Another limitation is that objects are seen from an aerial viewpoint, which sacrifices the experiential quality eyelevel perspective drawings offer.

Just as with perspectives, plans, and sections, different line weights represent the various elements of a paraline drawing. Line weights are used to make a distinction between spatial edges and planar corners. Profiling the outline of the building with a heavy line indicates the depth of its separation from its surrounding context. The lines of secondary importance and weight are other spatial edges within the building's outline—other edges that separate an object from its background. Then come the planar corners—lines that indicate the intersection of two surfaces, both of which can be seen—including the planar corners where the exterior walls of the building intersect the ground plane. Although these lines should be drawn lightly, they do convey spatial information, and to indicate this they should be drawn

slightly heavier than surface lines. The lightest lines are those that carry no spatial information and just lie on the surfaces of planes. As mentioned previously, this type of line includes tile joints and other textural indications such as wood grain or carpet texture.

Paraline drawings are easiest to understand if we apply a three-dimensional axis (x, y, z) system to them. A vertical axis indicates height, and the two horizontal axes, at 90 degrees to each other, indicate width and depth. The common rules for all paraline drawings are: all vertical lines are drawn as vertical in the drawing; all parallel lines are drawn parallel to each other; and all lines parallel to the three orthogonal axes are directly measurable.

In general, just about any building can be drawn as a paraline drawing, but you need a few additional instructions for special cases. Nonaxonometric lines (lines not parallel to one of the principal axes) do pose a slight problem when they do not occur in a plane that is parallel to the picture plane. The easiest way to draw these lines is to locate their ends and then connect those points. To determine those points, enclose the irregular shape within a box based on the orthogonal framework. You can then scale directly along its edges to locate the ends of the nonaxonometric lines. You should also note that these axonometric lines are not directly measurable.

Circles and curves also pose a problem. Circles occurring in planes not parallel to the picture plane appear as ellipses. A last problem we encounter is that long, receding dimensions often appear grossly exaggerated. To correct this you can proportionally reduce the scale of all dimensions in the direction that seems exaggerated, or you can choose a different view or even a different type of paraline drawing.

The two kinds of paraline drawings are isometric and oblique; both are aerial views. Isometric drawings view all three planes at the same angle, which results in a close approximation of reality but requires that every line be measured. Obliques select one plane to be drawn or traced to scale, with the other two planes seen at an angle. This saves time but allows distortion.

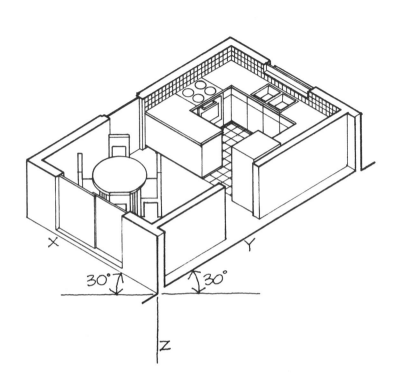

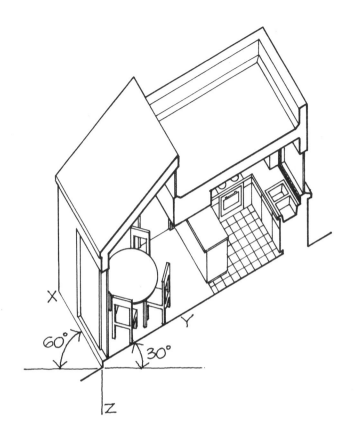

ISOMETRICS

The isometric paraline places equal importance on all three visible surfaces. It is as if we were viewing the corner of a cube at such an angle that all three lines radiating from the corner were at equal angles from each other. The isometric is constructed by drawing all vertical lines of the object as vertical and all lines in the two principal horizontal directions at 30-degree angles from the horizontal. The isometric is the least distorted of the paraline drawings. However, it is time-consuming to lay out because orthographic plans, sections, and elevations cannot be used to construct it and therefore all dimensions must be scaled during the drawing process. The isometric is also the least flexible of the paraline drawings because it is impossible to emphasize one of the three planes over the other two.

OBLIQUES

Oblique paraline drawings have one visible face (principle plane) parallel to the picture plane, which is represented in true proportion and scale. The other two orthographic surfaces are drawn at oblique angles to this principle surface. Any of these orthographic surfaces, whether horizontal or vertical in nature, can be used as the principle plane. The one you choose to use as the principle plane depends on what you wish to show. In the example above, the floor plane is emphasized as the principle plane because it is the most interesting and carries the most information. The biggest advantage of the oblique paraline drawing is that you can use orthographic views not only to make the construction of the drawing easier, but also to show the principle plane and all planes parallel to it to scale and in their true shape, proportion, and sizes.

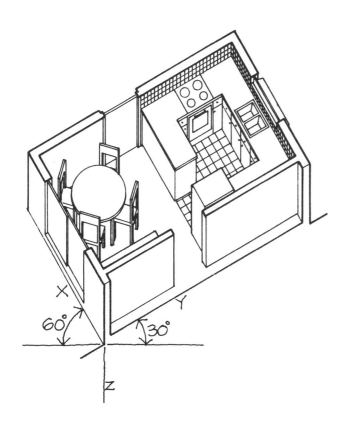

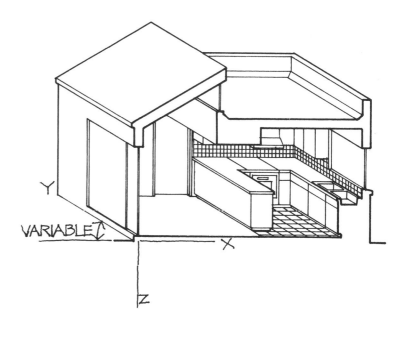

PLAN OBLIQUES

In plan obliques a horizontal plane or ground serves as the principle plane and is parallel to the picture plane. All the horizontal planes are drawn to scale and to their true shape, proportion, and size. This is the biggest advantage in using plan obliques, as circles, for example, can be drawn as true circles. Plan obliques depict a higher angle of view than isometric drawings and place more emphasis on horizontal surfaces than vertical surfaces. There are two common methods of constructing plan obliques. Vertical lines are drawn as vertical in both methods, but the horizontal axes have different orientations (45 degree/45 degree or 30 degree/60 degree). The method you choose depends upon which angle of view you want and the type of emphasis you want to place on the vertical surfaces.

ELEVATION OBLIQUES

In elevation obliques, a vertical plane (either a building elevation or the vertical plane of a section) serves as the principle plane and remains parallel to the picture plane. All vertical planes are drawn to scale and to their true shape, proportion, and size. All horizontal lines perpendicular to the picture plane are represented by lines drawn at an angle. The elevation oblique has a tendency to appear distorted, as is evident in the drawing above, making the proportional reduction of depth advisable. In order to avoid distortions do not use an angle under 30 degrees or over 60 degrees. Orthographic plans and sections can be used directly to construct the drawing. A major advantage of the elevation oblique is that it shows interior and exterior spaces as three-dimensional forms.

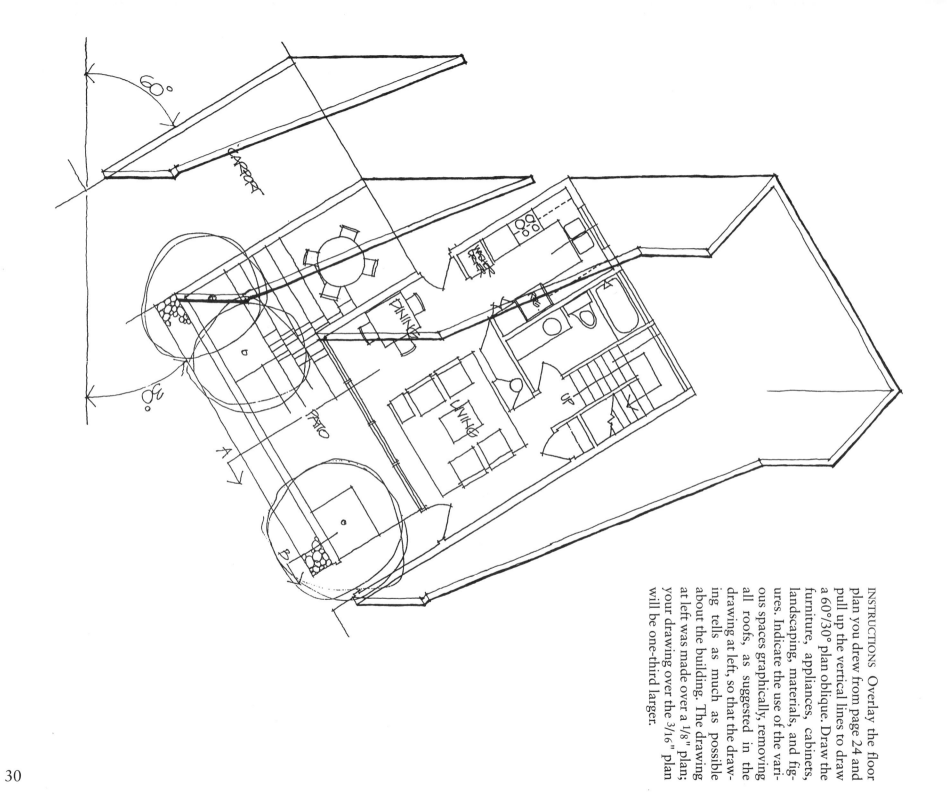

60°

CARPORT

30°

A

PATIO

DINING

KITCHEN

LIVING

UP

B

INSTRUCTIONS Overlay the floor plan you drew from page 24 and pull up the vertical lines to draw a 60°/30° plan oblique. Draw the furniture, appliances, cabinets, landscaping, materials, and figures. Indicate the use of the various spaces graphically, removing all roofs, as suggested in the drawing at left, so that the drawing tells as much as possible about the building. The drawing at left was made over a 1/8" plan; your drawing over the 3/16" plan will be one-third larger.

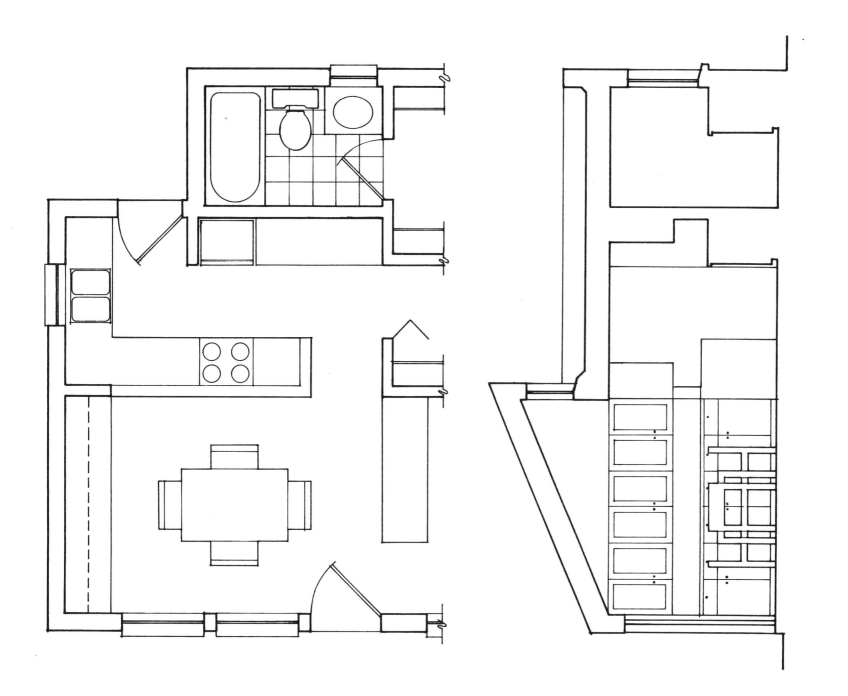

INSTRUCTIONS Draw two paraline drawings that demonstrate the spaces shown in the partial floor plan and the section above. Use two different types of paraline drawings: one that demonstrates the plan arrangement and one that demonstrates the vertical section. Use appropriate line weights to make the drawing readable.

Draw two paraline drawings, one showing the plan arrangement and one showing the vertical section, of the small office building shown in plan and section above. Choose the type of paraline drawing and the viewing angle that you feel would relate the most information about the building and its spaces. Use appropriate line weights to make the drawing readable.

3 Perspective (Subjective) Drawing

Perspectives are the only drawings that depict what the human experience of an environment will be after the environment is built. Since the quality of such experience should be a primary focus for environmental designers, we might expect that designers would begin drawing perspectives early and continue drawing them throughout their design process. Unfortunately, this is not the case. However, students must not be misled; if they wish to spend their professional apprenticeships as designers rather than production draftspersons, they must be able to make perspective sketches. I remember being made a junior designer and kept on through a big layoff because I could dependably produce perspective sketches.

Conventional perspective methods depend on laborious projection from a completed plan, so the tendency is to procrastinate about drawing perspectives until the plan is absolutely finalized. The problem is compounded by studio teachers who require the plan first and get caught up in a cycle of redesigning and recriticizing. By the time the lone perspective is drawn, it is no longer a design drawing, but is rather a presentation drawing, the design process having passed it by. Usually made in too little time and under too much pressure, the perspective drawing probably has no shadows or sense of light, little landscaping or furniture, ill-considered and awkwardly drawn materials, and few or no human figures helping to indicate the scale, function, and configuration of the space. Worst of all, the experience is so painful that the delineator vows to find some excuse for never drawing perspectives again. But the process doesn't have to be so tortuous. There must be a better way.

The rest of this book is devoted to making perspective drawings—subjective representations of environments to be experienced. The techniques are simple and direct, and, while learning them won't be effortless, it is certainly worth your effort if you want to be an environmental designer.

REPRESENTING A DESIGN AS AN ENVIRONMENT TO BE EXPERIENCED

In contrast to the objective separation of an orthographic drawing from its viewer, subjective drawings always include the viewer or subject. Eyelevel perspectives, especially interior perspectives, are the best subjective drawings because they surround the viewer and are representations of an environment rather than an object. The best subjective perspectives are taken from human eyelevel and represent the environment as it would appear to an occupant.

Perspectives have historically been accused of playing to the emotions and therefore being irrational in their appeal. The Royal Institute of British Architects refused, at one point, to accept perspectives in the building design competitions they sanctioned because they believed perspectives could be manipulated to flatter a design.

This special subjective involvement of the viewer is one of the desirable qualities of perspectives as representational drawings. Designers should want that kind of representation for their designs; not only will it help to sell the design and secure the necessary approvals to proceed, but hopefully also will foster a continuing and growing emotional involvement with the design of the building, garden, or interior.

The early representation of the design as a surrounding environment is the best way, in the relatively brief time of the design process, that the designer, the consultants, the client, and all those directly involved with the design can live with the design and realistically evaluate and improve it.

PERCEPTION

Traditionally, designers have been content to think of a drawing technique in terms of the media used to create it. This habit is inherited from art, where courses of many curricula are still described as "watercolor" or "oil painting." This chemical way of describing and thinking about graphic communication makes very little sense for designers. Unless we make a deliberate effort to develop better ways of thinking about drawing techniques, we will continue thinking about drawings in terms of media.

A much more basic way of thinking about drawing techniques is to classify them according to how they represent the way we perceive the environment. The work of psychologist James J. Gibson has made it clear that we perceive the environment through seeing and understanding its surfaces and edges.

The most basic division of drawing techniques, then, is into *edge* drawings and *surface* drawings. If the surfaces are to be of slick and characterless materials, there is no point in choosing a drawing technique that demands the rendering of all the surfaces. If, on the other hand, the environment is to have rich materials or needs strong shadows or subtle light distinctions, it would be advantageous to pick such a technique.

Surface drawings and edge drawings are also polar opposites in terms of realism and abstraction. Surface drawings are similar to the way we actually perceive the world. Like a black-and-white photograph, they are compositions of surfaces that, because of their various relationships to the sun or other sources of illumination, reflect different intensities of light. Edge drawings do not render surfaces but simply draw a line at every planar intersection or spatial discontinuity. While there are not really lines on the edges of things in the environment, the lines of an edge drawing communicate reality by indicating the foreshortening and overlapping of shapes.

SURFACE (TONE) DRAWING

Our perception of space begins with the perception of a continuous background surface. Throughout our evolutionary history, the earth's surface has always formed the lower half of our visual field, and it is only in relation to this continuous background surface that we are able to judge the size and distance of objects.

The most realistic way of representing an environment in a drawing is to render the tones and textures of *all* the surfaces that make up the environment. No edge lines are drawn in the pure form of this technique; only a difference in reflected light (or what we will call tone), indicates the edges. This representation of the world demands a great deal of time and skill.

EDGE (LINE) DRAWING

There are two kinds of edges: the simple edge that occurs when two surfaces intersect in such a way that both surfaces are visible, and the edge that defines the spatial relationship between two separate forms. Fundamentally different from the edge of an intersection of surfaces, the second kind of edge is linked to our evolutionary survival and our kinesthetic experience of space. These edges hide space—our enemies have appeared from behind them just as we have used them as hiding places. These are the edges that, when we move through the environment, move against their backgrounds, progressively revealing or concealing more of the world and conveying the kinesthetic experience of space.

Simple line drawings can represent both kinds of edges, and if line drawings are profiled to make the distinction described above, they can be remarkably efficient representations of the environment.

COMBINING EDGE AND SURFACE DRAWING

This technique, called line-and-tone drawing, combines surface and edge drawing and is advocated here as the basic drawing technique for designers. It has three strong advantages over surface and edge drawing:

1. It directly, simply, and equally represents the two perceptual clues we use to perceive the environment.
2. Unfinished, line-and-tone drawings are more manageable, flexible, and forgiving than either line drawings or tone drawings.
3. It is more humble, calls less attention to itself as a technique and to the skill of the delineator, and therefore interferes less with the design communication.

DRAWING TECHNIQUES

The subject of drawing technique never arises with orthographic drawings because they are usually drafted line drawings. Perspective drawing, however, demands that we understand the various techniques in which they can be drawn. Designers must master these techniques so they can choose which is most appropriate for each drawing. Having the freedom to choose a particular technique comes only with such an understanding and mastery. The assignments that follow are designed to introduce you to different drawing techniques and reproduction processes, so you can begin to diversify your drawing ability. If you can only draw one way you have no choice at all!

Understanding the differences between techniques is important because they vary dramatically in the skill and time they require, in the cost and difficulty of reproducing them, and, most basically, in the way they represent the environment. The range of variation has also recently broadened with reproduction techniques or "reprographics." Be sure that you can draw and use reproduction techniques in several different ways and with equal confidence.

The following pages demonstrate a complete categorization of the pure forms of the various techniques, based on the way they represent surfaces and edges and whether they are drawn on white or middletone paper. The rules should operate simply as guidelines for your experimentation with each technique.

I based the time and difficulty ratings on my own experience with techniques. It is important to keep track of how many hours it takes you to make similar drawings in the various techniques and to not judge a technique on only a single drawing experience. You should consider the various techniques only after you have tried them on different kinds of drawings in different situations, including one in which you have plenty of time to complete the drawing. Trying an unfamiliar technique for the first time under pressure is an almost sure-fire prescription for failure.

Although I believe it is of secondary importance in classifying drawing techniques, I should tell you which media were used in the following drawings. The lines were all drawn in India ink with technical pens of various sizes. The dark tones were made with a black Prismacolor™ pencil and the light tones on middletone paper were made with a white Prismacolor™ pencil. You or your teacher may wish to choose different pencils or pens. Ordinary soft-lead pencils also work well for dark tones and there are many fine-tip felt markers that can make lines. The only drawback with markers is that in time the fluids may bleed beyond the original lines or fade almost completely.

LINE ——————————

- spatial edges and planar corners defined with lines
- surfaces unrendered

time factor: 1 (on a scale of 1–10)
skill factor: 1

LINE—SPATIALLY PROFILED ——————————

- spatial edges and planar corners defined with lines
- spatial edges profiled—the farther an edge lies in front of its background the heavier the line should be, but its heaviness should be lightened in proportion to its distance from the viewer
- surfaces unrendered

time factor: 1½
skill factor: 1

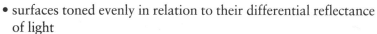

TONE

- surfaces toned evenly in relation to their differential reflectance of light
- spatial edges and planar corners defined by a change in tone—no lines
- stroking direction should respond to vertical or horizontal orientation of the surfaces, with the horizontal stroking always going toward the farthest vanishing point
- surface tones may be graduated within the surface to heighten contrasts with other tones at the surface's edges

time factor: 9
skill factor: 9

TONE-OF-LINES

- surfaces toned in relation to their differential reflectance of light
- tones made up of evenly spaced lines
- spatial edges and planar corners defined by a change in line spacing—no spatial edge lines
- direction of lines should respond to vertical or horizontal orientation of the surfaces, with horizontal lines always going toward the farthest vanishing point

time factor: 10
skill factor: 7

LINE-AND-TONE

- spatial edges and planar corners defined with lines
- spatial edges profiled—the farther an edge lies in front of its background the heavier the line should be, but its heaviness should be lightened in proportion to its distance from the viewer
- surfaces toned evenly in relation to their differential reflectance of light
- stroking direction should respond to vertical or horizontal orientation of the surfaces, with the horizontal stroking always going toward the farthest vanishing point

time factor: 7
skill factor: 4

LINE-AND-TONE ON MIDDLETONE

- spatial edges and planar corners defined with lines
- spatial edges profiled—the farther an edge lies in front of its background the heavier the line should be, but its heaviness should be lightened in proportion to its distance away from the viewer
- surfaces toned evenly in relation to their differential reflectance of light—black for shadow, white for sunlight, unrendered middletone paper for shade
- stroking direction should respond to vertical or horizontal orientation of the surfaces, with the horizontal stroking always going toward the farthest vanishing point

time factor: 7
skill factor: 4

EXERCISE INSTRUCTIONS

Each of the four tracing paper sheets that follow has a pair of drawings that will let you render the same drawing in two different techniques so you can experience their relative time and difficulty. It should be interesting to compare how long it takes to finish each drawing—remember that drawing in an unfamiliar technique takes considerably longer than drawing in a technique you've used before.

In each case the drawing on the left is printed very lightly and is to be rendered in tone or tone-of-lines so that the printed lines serve only as guidelines and will disappear in the final drawing.

The right-hand drawing is intended to be spatially profiled and rendered in line-and-tone. Shadows (which will be covered in the section on shadow-casting, page 81) are cast for you in order to make the finished drawings stronger.

These four experiences are printed on tracing paper so the finished drawings can be Diazo printed and colored or photocopied on middletone paper (see the section on reproduction techniques, page 128). This will help you to further understand the opportunities and problems inherent in the various reproduction techniques.

4 Handskills

Learning to draw depends on mastering a limited number of handskills. For environmental designers these skills are, thankfully, simplified as well as limited: of the many complicated things to draw in this world, our list includes only human figures in static poses, trees and plants, furniture, and, occasionally, automobiles. The delineation of this limited set of entourage is also deliberately simplified so that it never competes with the environment being represented.

Although these handskills may seem superficial compared to the main goals of design drawing, their mastery will free your conscious mind to generate, evaluate, and refine ideas (which is what the human mind does best) rather than struggle with how to draw the necessary figures, trees, and furniture.

The purpose of the following exercises is to introduce students to the most basic handskills needed to make professional-looking design drawings. Any employer will appreciate your mastery of the skills that follow. Most practicing professionals literally won't let you work on their drawings unless you have developed these skills, especially lettering!

This kind of drawing is direct copying; it's not particularly creative and is more like learning to spell. In today's society, repetitive drill is seldom required, except in athletics, music, drama, and dance, but basic graphic skills are traditional and beneficial for the design professions and can only be mastered by repeated practice. Later you will develop your own way of lettering, drawing trees, figures, furniture, and adding tones, but a good way to begin is to directly copy one way of drawing these basic graphic indications.

You will also find that the mastery of these few handskills will boost your appreciation not only of your own drawings, but also of your professional self-image and, most importantly, your enjoyment of drawing.

FROM UNCONSCIOUS INCOMPETENCE TO UNCONSCIOUS COMPETENCE

The kind of learning involved in mastering the handskills—and in understanding the advantages of their mastery—can be made clear by remembering how we all struggled to learn to tie our shoelaces.

Before we knew how to tie our shoes (before the days of Velcro™) we were in the blissful state of unconscious incompetence. We didn't know how to tie our shoes, but we weren't aware of our ignorance.

Then, one day our mother or father told us that we were old enough to learn how to tie our own shoes, pushing us into the very painful awareness of our ignorance, the state of conscious incompetence, which design students encounter the first time they have to present their designs in drawings and are made aware of the fact that there are many things they don't know how to draw very well.

For quite a while after that we struggled with fumbling fingers and failed knots until the day when, with the greatest concentration, we could successfully tie our shoelaces. We had reached conscious competence.

Today we have progressed far beyond that, to the state where we can tie our shoes while doing two or three other, more important, things without even thinking about it. We have to reach this point of unconscious competence with our handskills, too, so that our conscious minds can focus on more important issues.

LETTERING

ABCDEFGHIJKLMNOPQRSTUVWXYZ

THIS SPACE IS INTENDED
BEAM
COLUMN
TREAD
RISER

ABCDEFGHIJKLMNOPQRSTUVWXYZ

TO BE FILLED IN WITH WORDS
FOOTING
PILASTER
SHEAR
BENDING

ABCDEFGHIJKLMNOPQRSTUVWXYZ

FROM THE PROFESSIONAL
NAVE
APSE
TRANSEPT
AMBULATORY

ABCDEFGHIJKLMNOPQRSTUVWXYZ

VOCABULARY
MULLION
JAMB
SILL

Lettering is perhaps the most basic handskill and an analogy for all the others. You need to master several different alphabets so that you will always have a choice. Be aware of every lettering style's special character, relative difficulty, and degree of neutrality or "transparency."

INSTRUCTIONS You may letter this exercise with either a pen or graphite pencil, but if you use a pencil, use an H lead or softer and bear down hard enough to make clear, confident black strokes. Don't be a timid letterer. Although you're bound to make some wayward lines, bold strokes are actually easier to control.

50

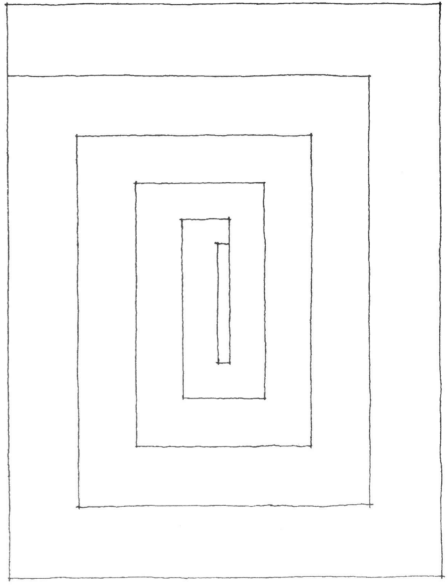

In tone and line-and-tone drawings you need to apply pencil tones in a disciplined way. The technique suggested here is to apply the tones at 45 degrees with a black Prismacolor™ pencil. Such a technique can add great unity and consistency to your drawings, much like the quality contributed by the grain of any unpainted wooden object.

INSTRUCTIONS Left side: Make the concentric bands progressively darker, beginning with an outer band of very light gray and progressing in equal steps to a very dark inner band. Leave the central rectangle white. It should look whiter than the surrounding paper. Right side: Make the continuous spiral band progressively darker as it winds toward the center, again leaving the small central rectangle white.

FIGURES

INSTRUCTIONS Draw the figure groups (similar, but of your own invention) in a progression from top to bottom. Beginning with the small, very sketchy figure groups of the top row, add refinement and detail so that the larger groups in the middle and especially on the bottom are fully detailed, with clothing, hair, and hands. You may even find it interesting to add some props that tell something more about the people: their ages, their occupations, or their relationships to one another. Don't forget to spatially profile or outline the figure groups. Surround each group with a heavier boundary line. Use page 66 as a reference.

TREES, PLANTS, AND GROWIES

INSTRUCTIONS Imagine that this is the display area of a commercial nursery and fill it with as many kinds of trees, shrubs, and ground cover as possible. Refer to pages 58 and 59 and to books on entourage in your library. Choose the trees, plants, and ground cover that you can draw most successfully and try to master the drawing of two or three kinds of them.

FURNITURE

INSTRUCTIONS Imagine that this drawing represents a large furniture showroom. Fill it with as many different pieces of furniture as possible, with figure groups to demonstrate the use of the pieces of furniture. Refer to page 62 and current furniture advertisements for ideas. Don't forget to include beds, dressers, and entertainment centers. Use subdivisions and multiples of the 30" cube to lay out the furniture (page 63).

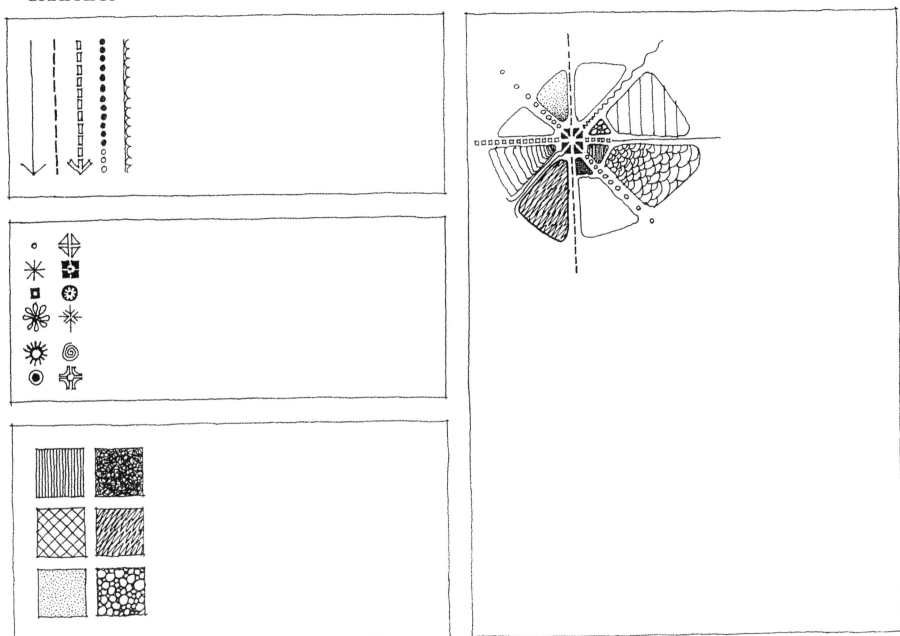

The most basic graphic elements are points, lines, and areas. These each offer a wide range of graphic alternatives that can be assigned various qualitative meanings. You need to develop a vocabulary that includes several variations for each indication.

INSTRUCTIONS On the left-hand side, practice the variations shown and add some of our own. On the right-hand side, combine the various graphic indications in diagrammatic compositions. You may imagine the diagrams are maps, plan-view functional diagrams, site analyses, football plays, or city plans.

55

TEACHING IT BACKWARDS:
A PSYCHOLOGICAL APPROACH

After forty years of trying to help architecture students learn to draw freehand perspectives, I have concluded that we usually teach it backwards. We teach perspective drawing in a *logical* order when we should teach it in a *psychological* order.

Perspective drawing is usually taught in the same order in which any perspective is made. We teach students first to lay out the perspective, then to cast shadows, and then to indicate the materials and add the landscaping, furniture, and figures. This seems the obvious, logical approach.

The problem is that the traditional method for drawing perspectives is so complicated that we never even get around to shadow-casting, let alone adding materials and entourage.

The result is that when students try to apply what they have learned in drawing class to the perspective drawing they are doing in their design studio, they fail miserably. Even if they save enough time and can remember how to plan-project the perspective, they won't be able to cast shadows or add textures, landscaping, furniture, and figures to make the drawing come alive. Instead of enjoying making the one drawing that shows the three-dimensional reality of their design, they leave it a barren wire-frame drawing or, if they are brave enough to attempt adding shadows, materials, and entourage, they are rewarded with the crushing humiliation of watching themselves ruin their perspectives by adding bogus lights and darks and awful entourage to what should be the crowning communication of their design.

The final touches of a perspective may seem superficial or trivial to the design of the space, but to anyone trying to understand what the environment will look like when it is built, they are invaluable. And for the designer who makes the drawings, the ability to add the finishing touches is anything but superficial or trivial. Designers need to like their own drawings and enjoy the process of making them. The ability to finish a drawing strongly and surely may be one of the foundations of a designer's creative confidence as well as a source of great pleasure.

For these reasons I have turned the process around in my teaching, forsaking what seems to be the logical order of teaching perspective drawing in favor of a psychological order, which I have found to be more successful and humane.

After the basic techniques of drawing are understood, I begin helping students to master drawing the elements of additional interest and the materials of textural interest, as well as intelligently placing them in perspectives. Next I teach them to cast shadows in perspective and integrate the figures and furniture or landscaping with the shadow patterns, using the perspective structure to cast the shadows on given perspectives.

And last of all they learn to construct the perspective, cast the shadows, add the textural and additional interest, and enjoy the finishing touches of their perspective, which by now they are much better prepared to do.

I also insist that the perspectives be drawn freehand, beginning with their layout. The procedures demonstrated here certainly can be drafted, but if students pick up the T square and triangle and retreat into the pseudo-accuracy of drafting in laying out perspectives, they miss learning the confidence of being able to draw *anything* freehand, including perspective layouts. In my experience, the breaking of drafting dependency should be one of the most important goals of design-drawing courses.

In professional offices, one of the distinguishing marks of designers as opposed to draftspersons is that of all the people in the office, they tend to be the ones who can draw perspectives and use them early, continuously, and confidently in any design process. I don't believe this is a coincidence.

$\text{\textcircled{5}}$ Additional Interest: Drawing and Placing Entourage

Additional interest is the kind of interest that we or nature add to the built environment: trees, plants, furniture, and human figures. These elements can specify the scale, indicate the use, and demonstrate the space of an environment represented in a perspective. Their placement in a perspective should not hide space-defining intersections and they should never preempt the design of the environment by being self-consciously designed or drawn. The two best approaches are to draw completely characterless objects or specific, well-known models, so that they never compete with the design of the environment.

Many designers learn perspective layout and shadow-casting, or learn to produce computer-generated perspectives with the shadows cast, and still make dull, disappointing drawings because they never master the layer of freehand entourage that gives perspectives their character and helps them to read as real environments. One of the reasons for this failure may be that the delineation of entourage seems like so much arbitrary fluff in comparison to perspective and shadow-casting that demand logical step-by-step procedures.

I believe it is important to learn how to add material textures, figures, furniture, and trees and plants because I have noticed that students who master these apparently secondary and cosmetic finishing touches enjoy their drawings more. This means the self-enjoyment, self-improvement cycle that automatically and naturally improves drawing has begun.

Finishing a drawing requires two abilities: learning to draw textures and items of additional interest (see the chapter on handskills), and learning to place textures, figures, furniture, and trees and plants intelligently in perspectives.

The following set of exercises is designed to let students practice adding the finishing touches of a design drawing by selecting and placing items of additional interest in perspectives.

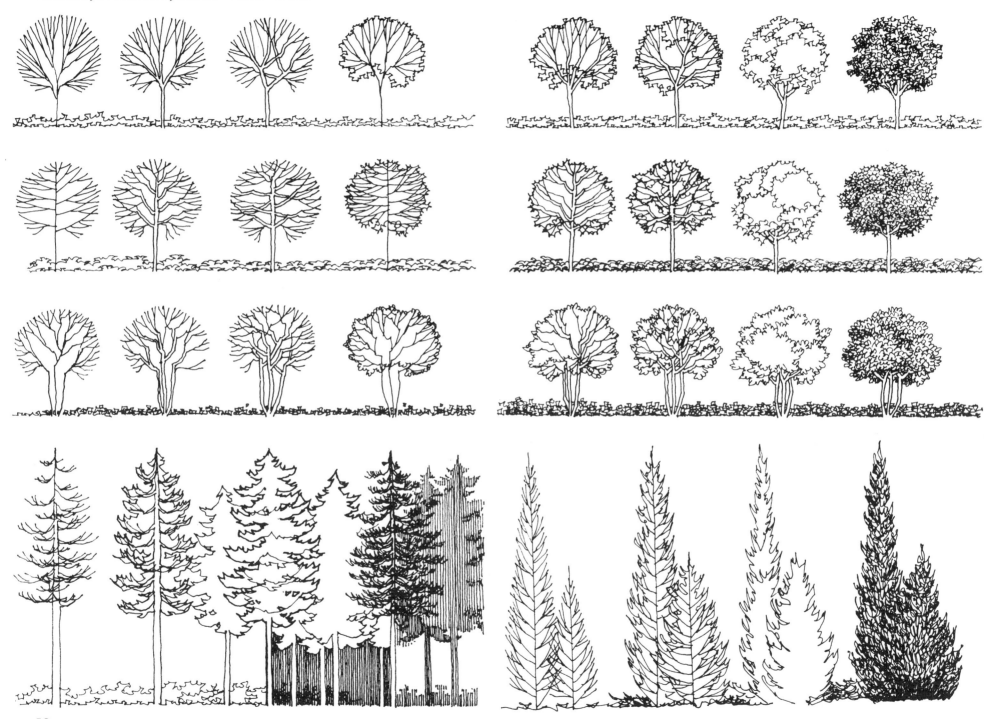

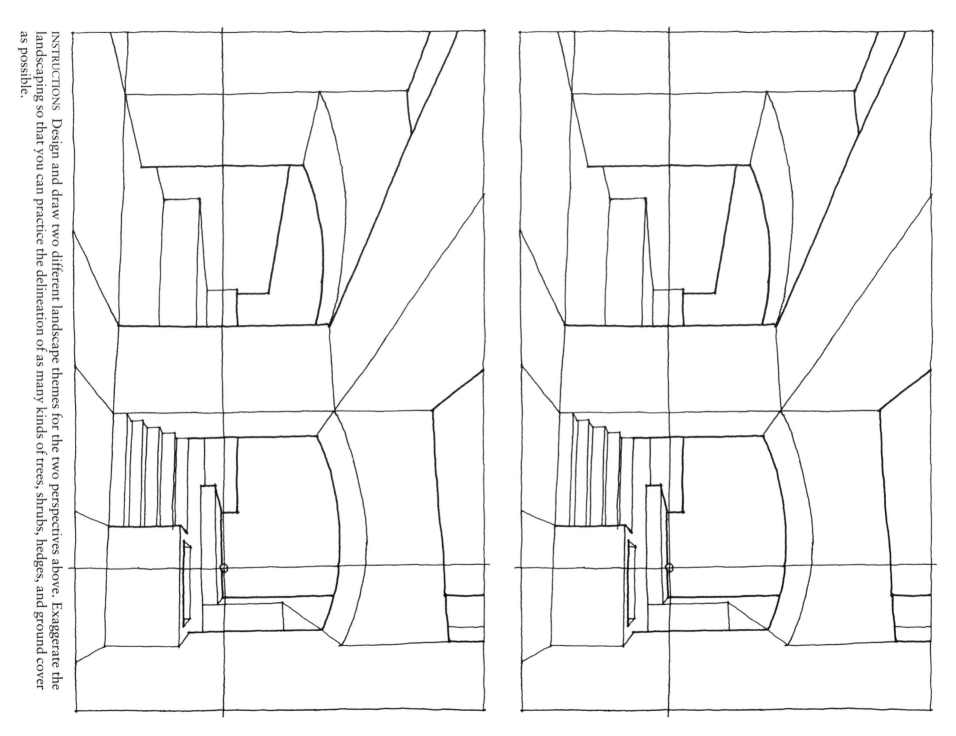

INSTRUCTIONS Design and draw two different landscape themes for the two perspectives above. Exaggerate the landscaping so that you can practice the delineation of as many kinds of trees, shrubs, hedges, and ground cover as possible.

60

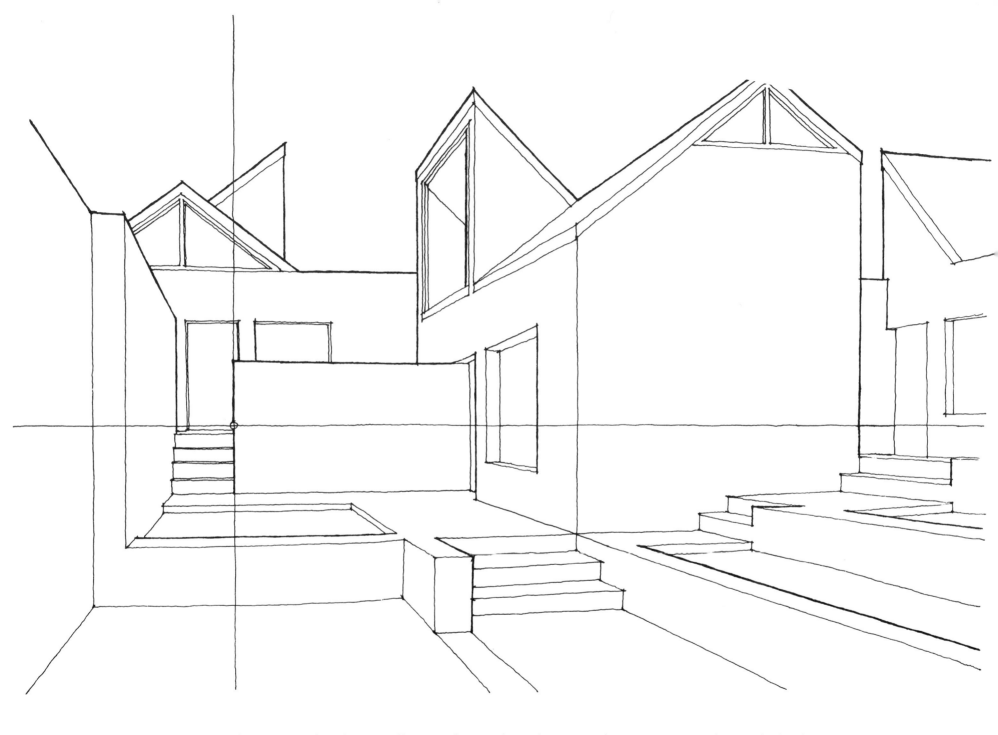

INSTRUCTIONS Landscape this space with a diverse collection of trees, shrubs, hedges, vines, and ground cover. If you want to keep the emphasis on the architecture, cast shadows only on and from the architecture. If you want to emphasize the landscape, cast shadows from the trees and plants and shade the sides of the trees and plants that are turned away from the sun.

61

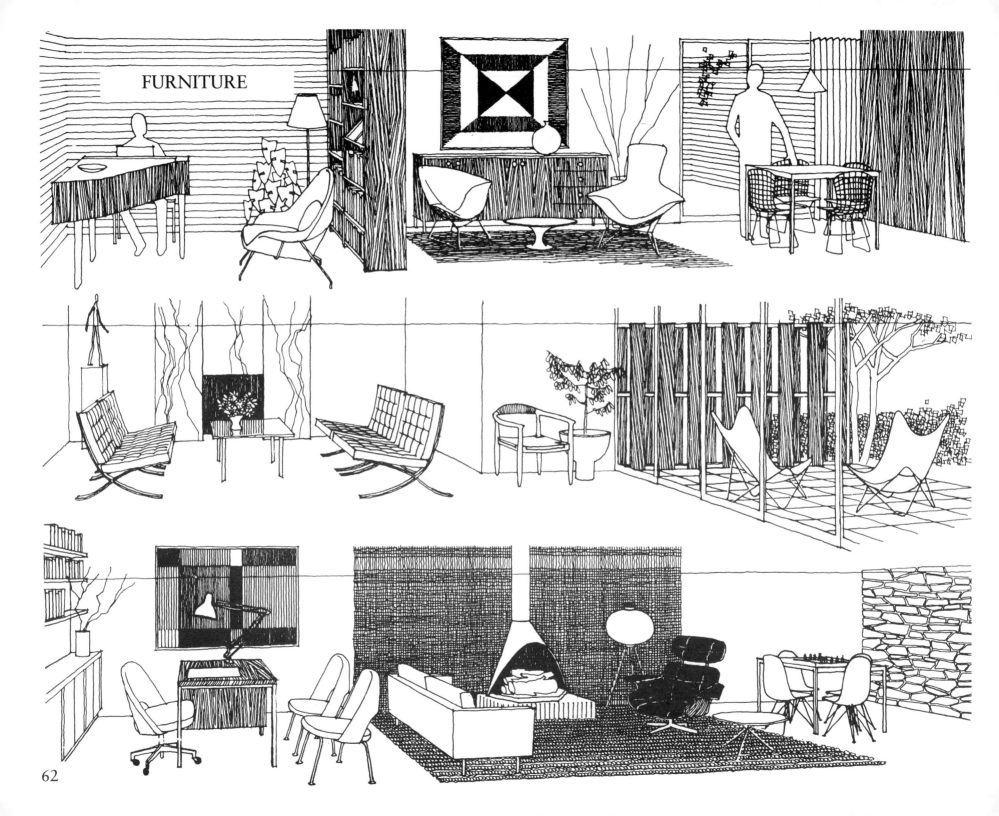

FURNITURE

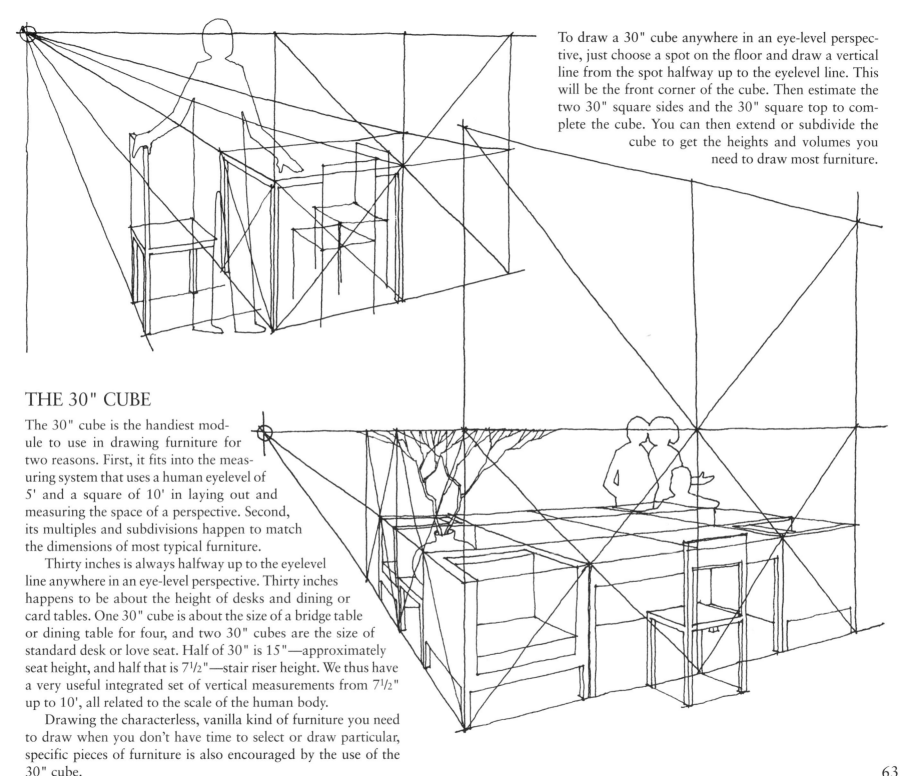

To draw a 30" cube anywhere in an eye-level perspective, just choose a spot on the floor and draw a vertical line from the spot halfway up to the eyelevel line. This will be the front corner of the cube. Then estimate the two 30" square sides and the 30" square top to complete the cube. You can then extend or subdivide the cube to get the heights and volumes you need to draw most furniture.

THE 30" CUBE

The 30" cube is the handiest module to use in drawing furniture for two reasons. First, it fits into the measuring system that uses a human eyelevel of 5' and a square of 10' in laying out and measuring the space of a perspective. Second, its multiples and subdivisions happen to match the dimensions of most typical furniture.

Thirty inches is always halfway up to the eyelevel line anywhere in an eye-level perspective. Thirty inches happens to be about the height of desks and dining or card tables. One 30" cube is about the size of a bridge table or dining table for four, and two 30" cubes are the size of standard desk or love seat. Half of 30" is 15"—approximately seat height, and half that is 7 1/2"—stair riser height. We thus have a very useful integrated set of vertical measurements from 7 1/2" up to 10', all related to the scale of the human body.

Drawing the characterless, vanilla kind of furniture you need to draw when you don't have time to select or draw particular, specific pieces of furniture is also encouraged by the use of the 30" cube.

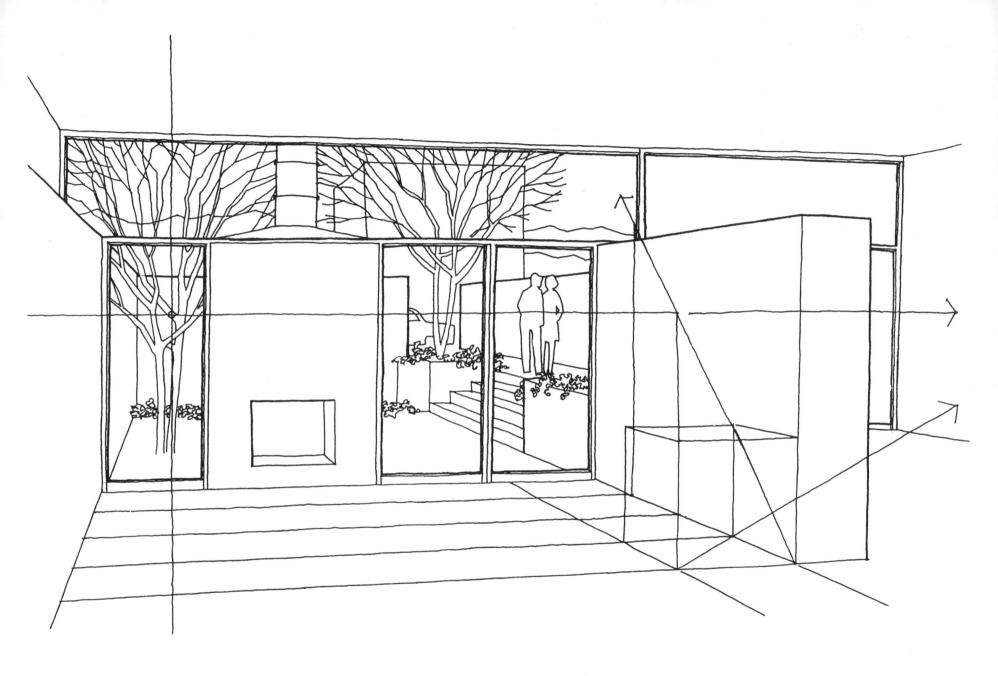

INSTRUCTIONS Design and draw a furniture arrangement for the space in the perspective above. The 30" cube is provided as the most useful module for drawing furniture, and you can project a 30" grid over the entire space by locating a vanishing point (VP) for floor diagonals on the eyelevel vanishing line (VL) where the arrows meet, to the right.

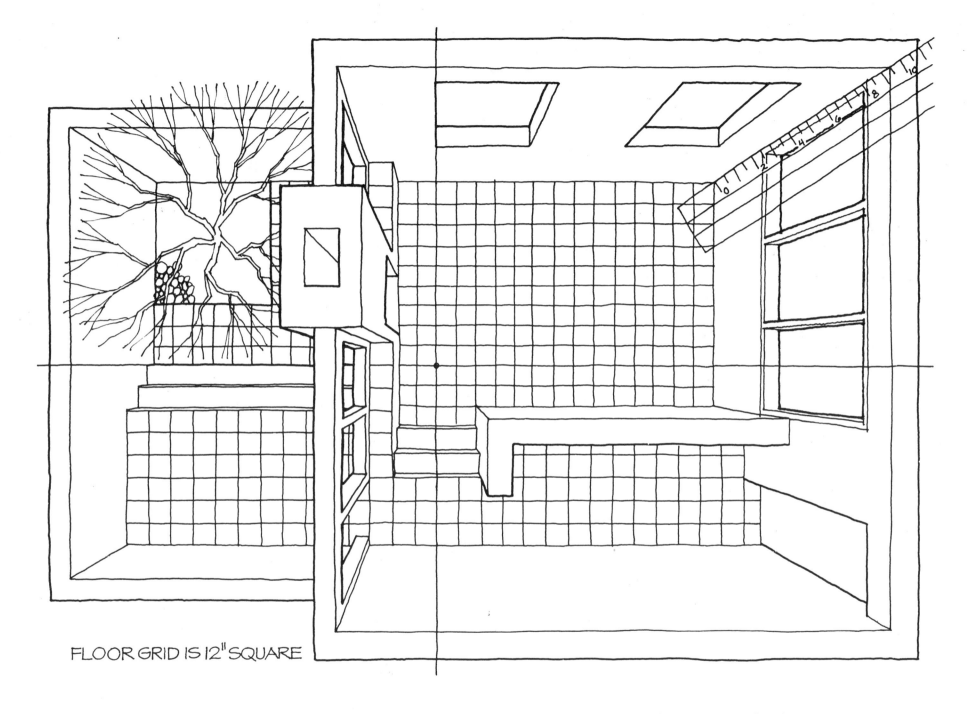

FLOOR GRID IS 12" SQUARE

INSTRUCTIONS Design and draw a furniture arrangement for the spaces in this aerial one-point perspective. Heights can be determined in the upper right-hand corner and projected around the perspective where they are needed (ignore any foreshortening). This is an effective way to study furniture arrangements and present them to clients.

65

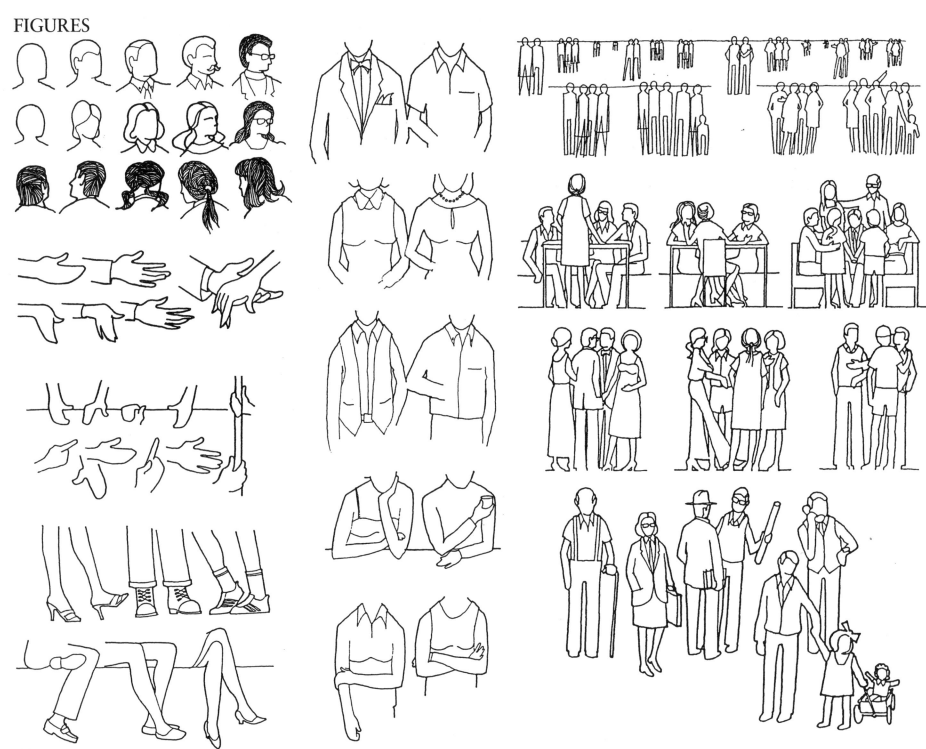

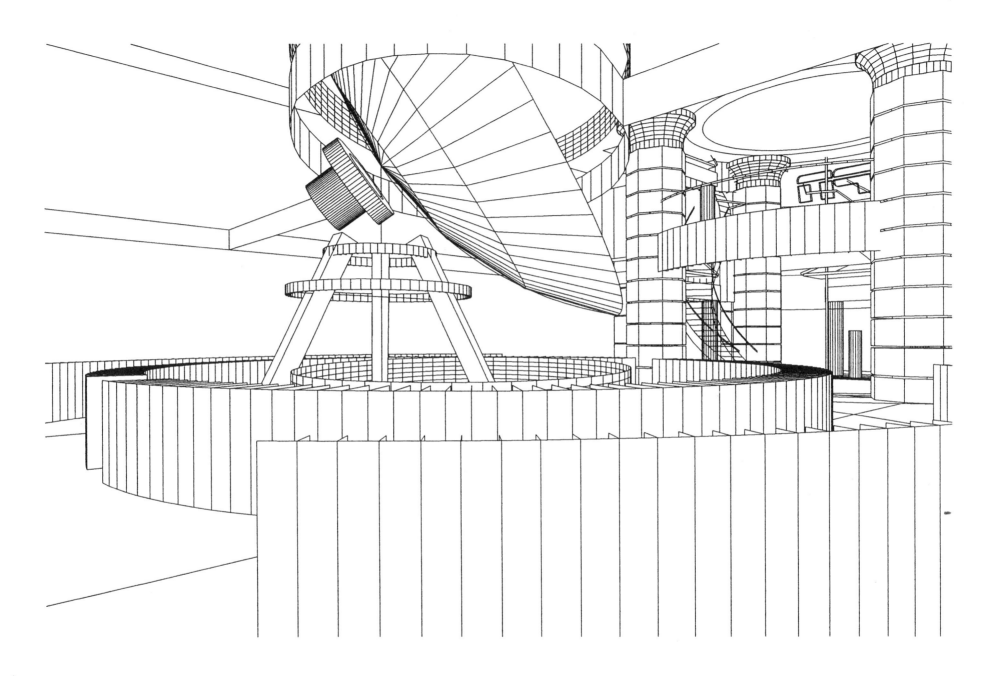

INSTRUCTIONS This is a computer wire-frame interior perspective of the mezzanine level of the sports bar shown on page 68. It needs figures and furniture to give it life and make it look as it will when completed and functioning on a busy night. Find the eye-level line and add figures seated around tables and at the circular bar. Add bartenders and a double band of big television monitors showing sporting events.

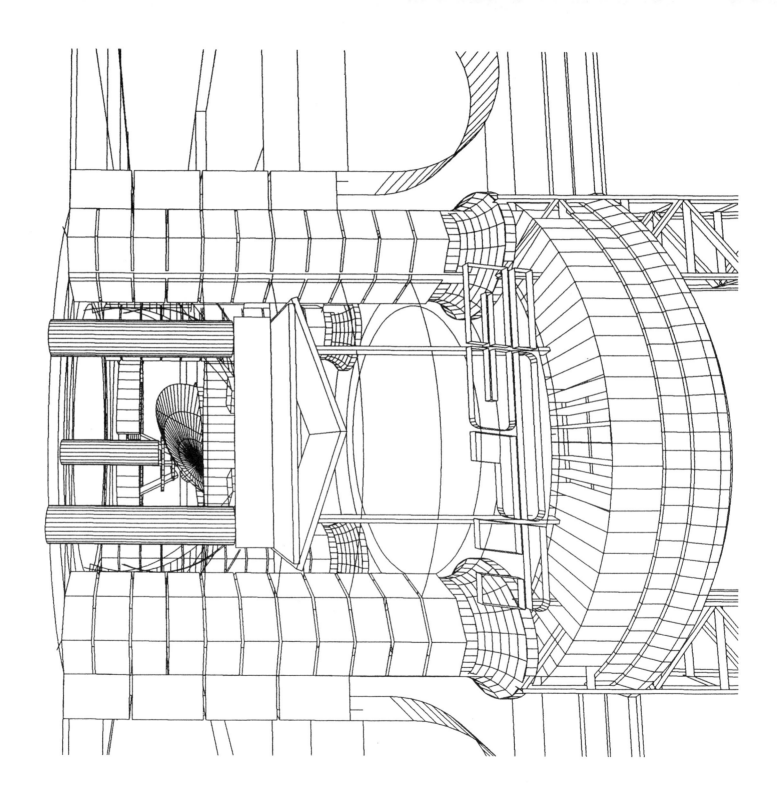

INSTRUCTIONS This is a computer wire-frame drawing of a proposed sports bar designed around a super satellite dish that receives the transmission of sporting events from around the world. Drawings like this need the addition of figures and furnishings to give them life and make them look real. Find the eyelevel line and add figure groups as well as furniture and a car at the curb.

68

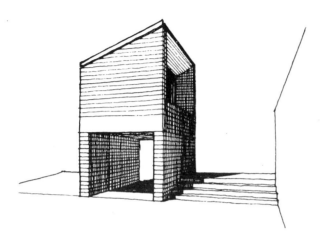

CONTEXT

You have to include the surrounding context of the building, garden, or interior you are designing when making representational drawings of any designed environment. It is useful to use landscape painting's three categories of foreground, middleground, and background. The building or garden usually occupies the middleground, while the foreground and background extend the space of the drawing and provide a realistic context. In perspectives of interiors, the interior itself may be both middleground and foreground, with only an exterior background context seen through windows and doors.

The extension of space in the background is easily accomplished by simply indicating layers of hedges, trees, buildings, or mountains that disappear and reappear from behind the building or through the windows of an interior.

The foreground is more difficult for two reasons. First, it must appear to lie down or recede into and out of the paper it is drawn on. This is best accomplished by drawing transverse horizontal textures (grass, hedges, walks, or ground contour lines) that get denser in the distance so that the ground plane appears to be a receding horizontal plane. The second problem is to articulate the space of the foreground without hiding the building, garden, or interior. This is best done with vertical objects (trees, light poles, or human figures) that are carefully placed to avoid the volume-defining corners of the design in the middleground.

The exercises that follow are designed to help students learn to indicate a realistic context for a building or environment. Everything you design will exist in a context and will be judged by its relationships to whatever surrounds it.

69

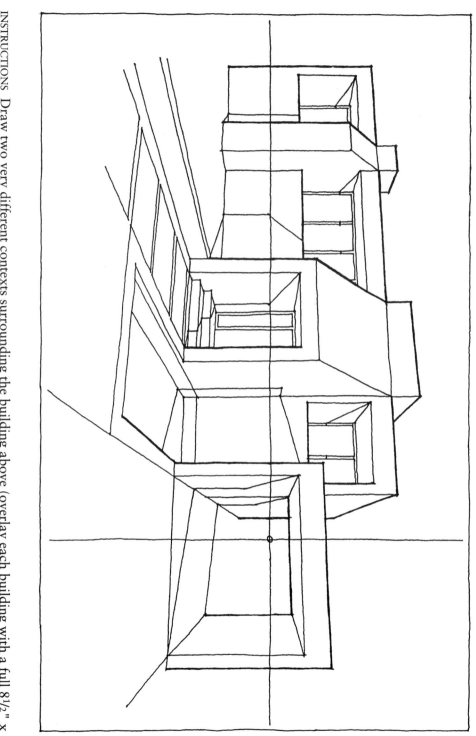
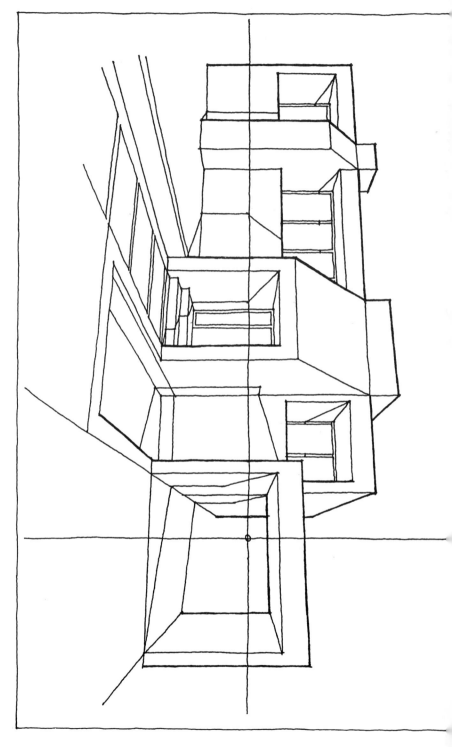

INSTRUCTIONS Draw two very different contexts surrounding the building above (overlay each building with a full 8½" x 11" sheet of paper if you need the room). Don't be afraid to draw trees in front of the building, but raise the leaf canopy so the building isn't obscured. Be sure to run all foreground textures transversely, not toward the near VP.

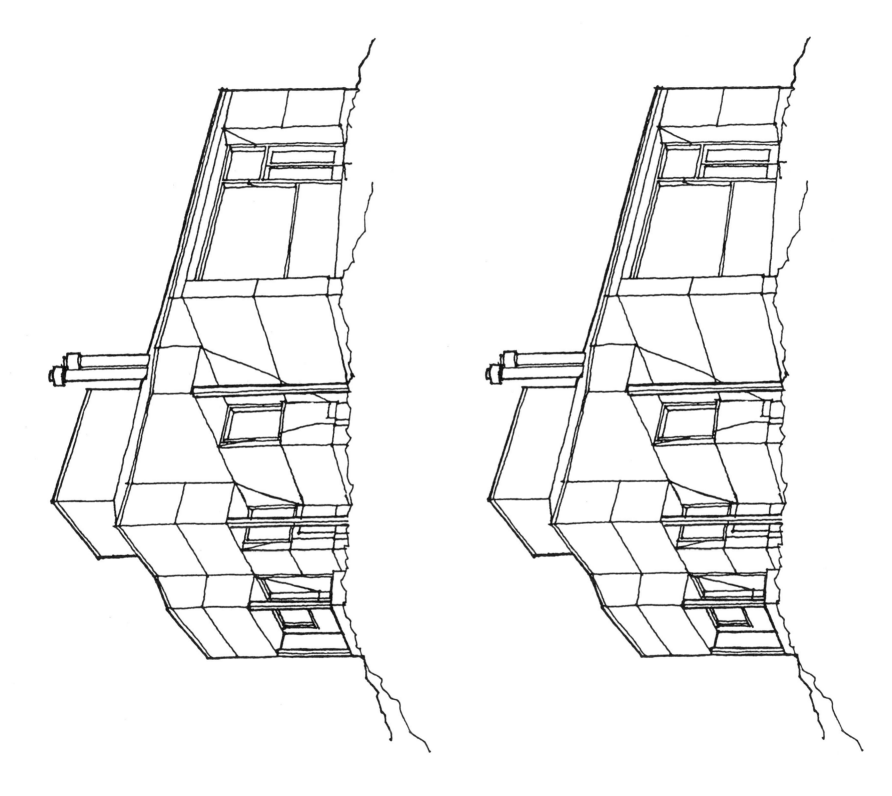

INSTRUCTIONS Draw two very different contexts surrounding the building above (overlay each building with a full 8½" x 11" sheet of paper if you need the room). Don't be afraid to draw trees in front of the building, but raise the leaf canopy so the building isn't obscured. Be sure to run all foreground textures transversely, not toward the near VP.

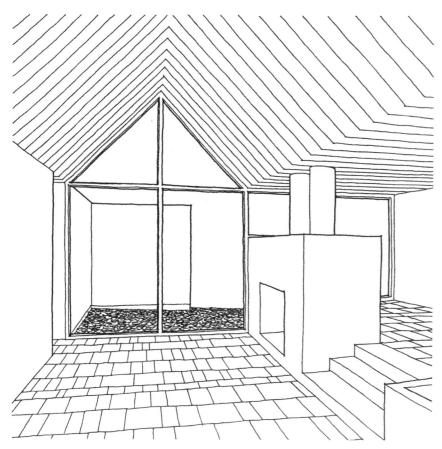

6 Textural Interest: Drawing and Placing Materials

Textural interest in a drawing is a curious combination of anticipated and remembered tactile experience. A good representational drawing can trigger the memory of the way a material feels. The main source of textural interest is in the materials of which any design is made. Designers should learn to draw the materials they propose to use both for themselves and their clients. Textural interest should always begin with a floor or ground texture as a continuous background surface that is the basis for spatial perception.

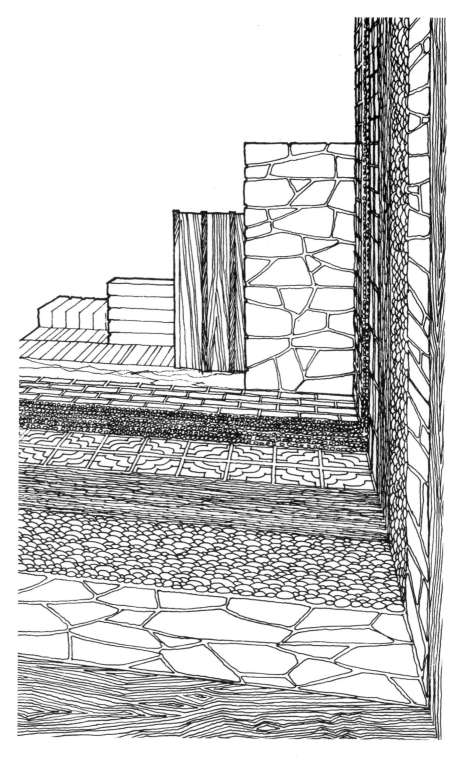

These experiences are designed to help students learn to render the specific materials of which their designs will be constructed and place them intelligently in a drawing. The visual and physical properties of an environment's materials are inseparable from the functional and sensory experience of that environment. Designers should learn to draw materials convincingly, especially those they most like to use in their buildings.

When drawing early sketches before final material selections have been made, it is wise to place the materials according to the human perception of space. Because our perception of space depends on a continuous background surface, beginning with the floor or ground surface, that's where we should place the first textures in a perspective. Further decisions on where to place textures depends on whether you are an architect, a landscape architect, or an interior designer. An architect should keep the textures on the space-defining architectural surfaces; a landscape architect might want to depict the textures of the plant materials in addition to floors, ground surfaces, and walls; and an interior designer might want to illustrate the textures of the furnishings.

Material selection and indication are very important in design and in design drawing. They provide textural and tactile interest both to drawings and environments, and they can indicate permanence and craftsmanship in the way they are selected and put together. One of the best ways to make your drawings realistic is to observe, learn, and draw the material's typical installation details: the chamfer strip on concrete corners, the various trim pieces for wood paneling, or the finishing of a brick wall with a rowlock course at the top.

INSTRUCTIONS Select and draw two quite different sets of related materials to develop your ability to draw a variety of materials and to experience the difference material choices can make in a building and in a drawing, Be careful in your choice of the mate- rial's directionality in perspective and be aware of the difficulty of drawing certain materials at a scale this small. Some materials are especially hard to draw on foreshortened surfaces like the right side of this building.

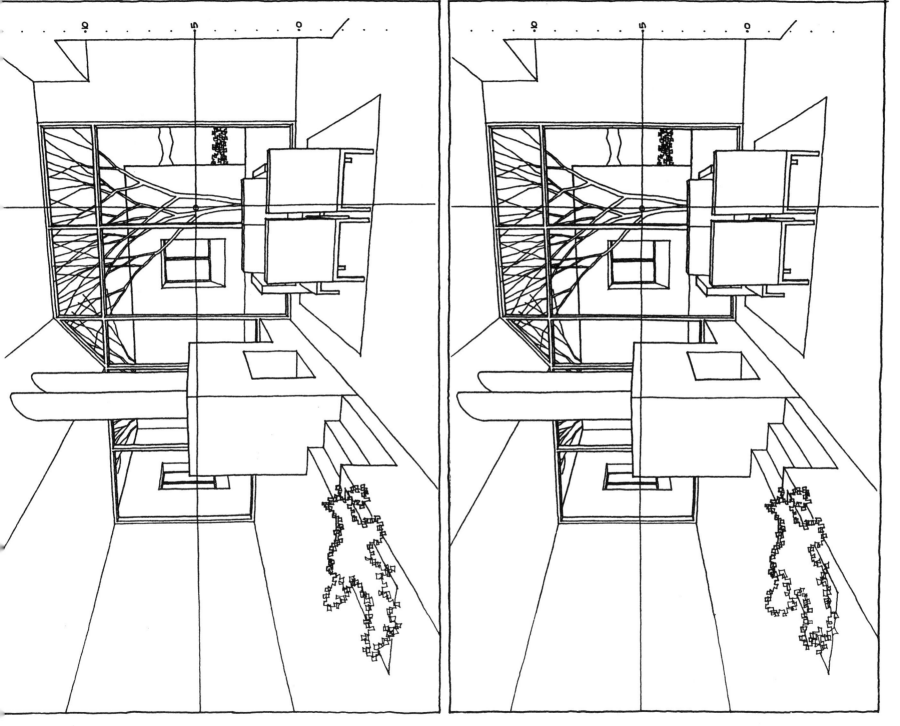

INSTRUCTIONS Select and draw two quite different sets of related materials of which to construct the interior space shown. Be careful in your choice of the material's directionality in perspective and be aware of the difficulty of drawing certain materials at a scale this small. Directional materials on horizontal surfaces like the floor or ceiling are more effective and easier to draw if they are transverse or crossways in their direction.

75

REFLECTIONS

The exercises that follow are designed to help students learn to draw reflections in glass, water, and other reflective materials. Reflectivity is often the strongest characteristic of a material and to render glass or water as either transparent or opaque is to misunderstand them as materials.

In perspective, whether a reflective surface is vertical, like glass usually is, or horizontal, like water always is, makes a big difference. Reflections on a vertical surface converge toward the VP that is perpendicular to the reflective surface and foreshorten accordingly. Reflections on a horizontal surface, on the other hand, do not converge or foreshorten. The two kinds of surfaces should also be rendered in a direction that helps them appear to be either vertical, like glass, or horizontal, like water.

GLASS REFLECTIONS

In drawing reflections in glass, there are two realms to be reflected. The first realm, which is that between the viewer and the glass, is seen twice—in reality and in its reflection. The second realm is all that is behind the viewer and is *only* seen in its reflection. The rules for drawing reflections in glass are:

- Pull everything that exists in front of the glass perpendicularly back through the glass.

- Draw these reflections as if they were the same distance (foreshortened) behind the glass as they actually are in front of the glass.

- Indicate all reflections on the glass with vertical tone-of-lines, since the reflecting surface is vertical.

- Tone reflections of objects between the viewer and the glass the same relative darkness or lightness they are in unreflected reality.

- Tone reflections of everything behind the viewer as progressively lighter layers of receding space.

WATER REFLECTIONS

Reflections on water are easier because there is only one reality reflected in the water's horizontal surface. There is no realm behind the viewer to be reflected, and the reflections neither converge nor foreshorten. The rules for drawing reflections in water are:

- Pull everything that exists above the surface of the water down through the water vertically.

- Draw these reflections as if they were the same distance below the water as they actually are above it.

- Use the same VPs to draw the reflections as were used to lay out the perspective.

- Indicate all reflections on the water with wavy transverse horizontal tone-of-lines, since the reflecting water surface is horizontal.

- Tone reflections with the same relative darkness or lightness they are in unreflected reality.

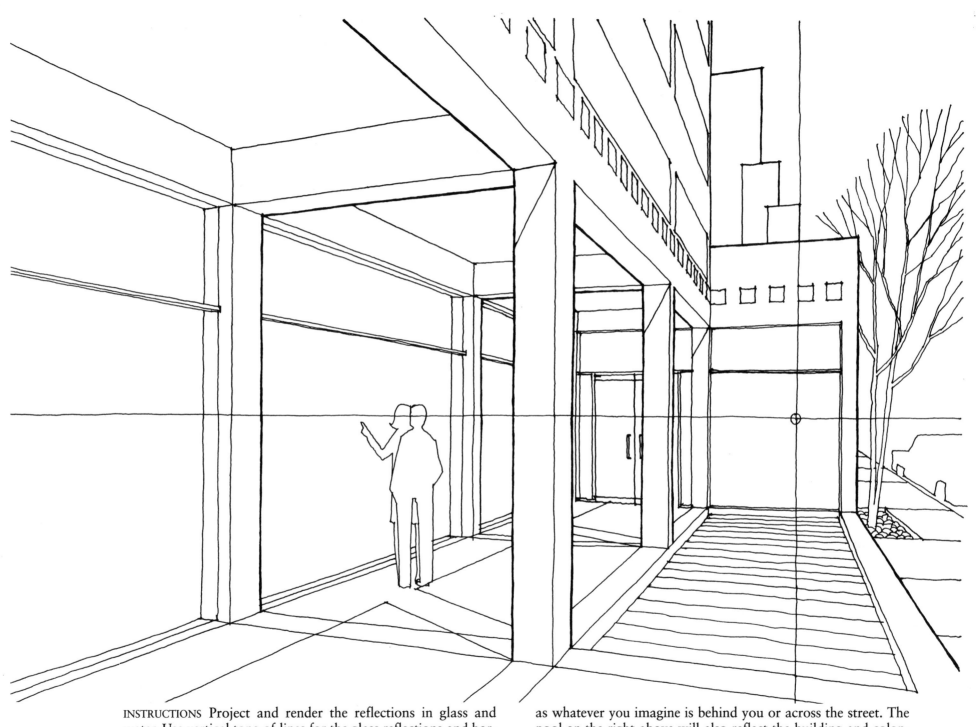

INSTRUCTIONS Project and render the reflections in glass and water. Use vertical tone-of-lines for the glass reflections and horizontal tone-of-lines for the water reflections. The entire first floor of the building is glass and will reflect the colonnade as well as whatever you imagine is behind you or across the street. The pool on the right above will also reflect the building and colonnade. Render the shadows, which are cast for you, and add figure groups, a fountain, materials, and urban street furniture.

78

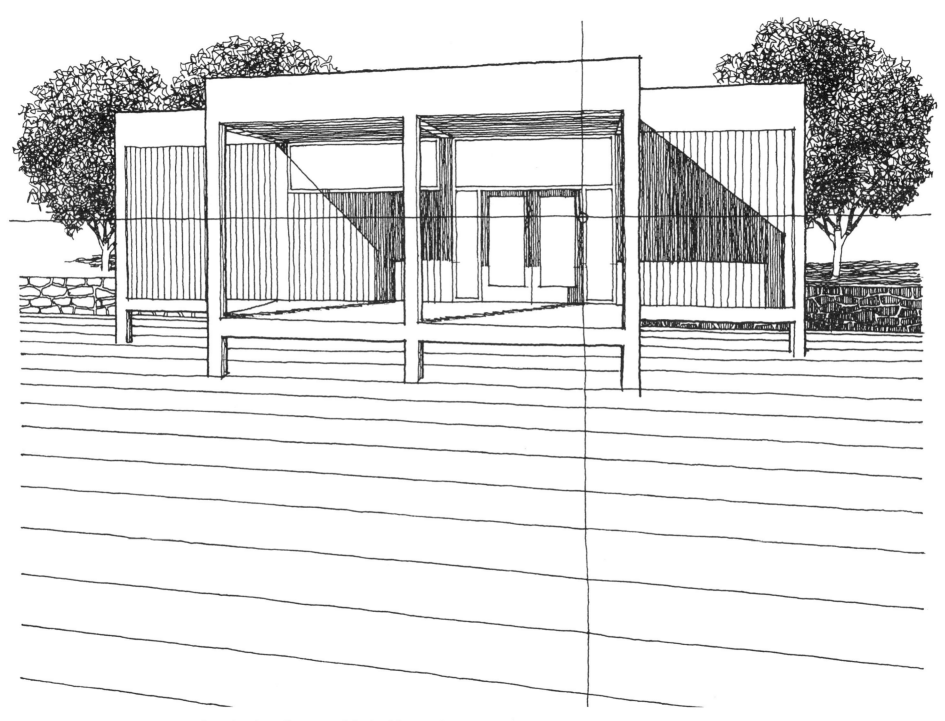

INSTRUCTIONS Project and render the reflections of the building in the lake and glass reflections of the porches, plus whatever you imagine to be behind you. Use vertical tone-of-lines for the glass reflections and horizontal tone-of-lines for the water reflections. Match the tones of the reflections to the building and expect to see much more of the undersides of the roof and floor in the reflections than in the building.

79

INSTRUCTIONS This exercise combines shadow-casting and reflections. Complete it after you have learned shadow-casting in chapter 7. Cast the shadows from the two perpendicular shadow angles given (arrows). Project and render the reflections in the covered swimming pool as a horizontal tone-of-lines. Make a careful light analysis of the ceiling, to be reflected in the water. The colonnade, with its sun, shade, and shadow, and the sky beyond should also be reflected, using white and nonphoto-blue Prismacolors™. Be sure to add furniture and other figure groups in and out of the pool.

80

The color coding in this section is a reminder of the first principle of perspective: that the three sets of parallel planes in a perspective converge to three separate VLs.

- Horizontal planes and the horizontal eyelevel VL into which they vanish are colored red.

- Near vanishing vertical planes and the near vertical VL into which they vanish are colored green.

- Far vanishing vertical planes and the far vertical VL into which they vanish are colored blue.

This understanding is necessary when finding VPs for sets of "perpendicular" lines.

7 Tonal Interest: Shadow-Casting in Direct Perspectives

Tonal interest is the most powerful of the interest categories, the last to be squinted out, and the one that can be seen from the greatest distance. Tonal interest depends on the full range of grays, from pure white to solid black, over broad areas of the drawing. The main source of tonal interest is light, shade, and shadow. Like spatial interest and textural interest, light, shade, and shadows are integral parts of any design. This set of experiences is designed to help students study alternative shadow patterns on the environments they are designing.

Shadow-casting is traditionally taught on plans, sections, and elevations from a fixed sun angle. It is much more useful to learn shadow-casting in three dimensions and to experience the freedom of placing the sun where you want and studying and choosing the most characteristic or dramatic shadow patterns.

Learning shadow-casting in perspective means that you will be using the same perspective structure used in drawing the perspective. While there are computer programs that, after you build a computer model of an environment, cast the shadows for you, you still need to learn to cast shadows in the precomputer conceptual drawings you make for yourself.

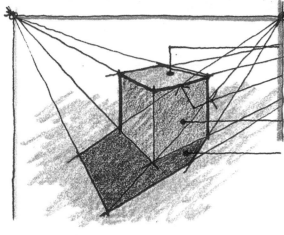

NOMENCLATURE

SUN: a surface lit directly by the sun

CASTING EDGE: any outside corner that separates sun and shade

SHADE: a surface turned away from the sun

SHADOW: a surface turned toward the sun except that an intervening mass blocks the sun's rays and casts a shadow; the casting edge of an object casts the boundary of the shadow

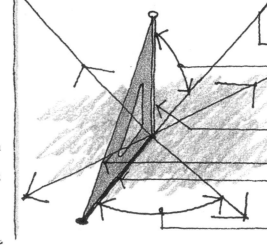

THE SUN'S RAY TRIANGLE

FLAGPOLE VP

VERTICAL ANGLE OF THE SUN: measured in the vertical plane rising out of the flag-pole shadow

FLAGPOLE : a vertical casting edge

SUN'S RAY: the hypotenuse

FLAGPOLE SHADOW: the ⊥ shadow cast on a horizontal surface by a vertical line

HORIZONTAL ANGLE OF THE SUN: measured on the earth's surface as an azimuth related to the compass points

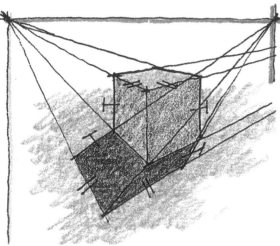

In rectangular environments there are only two possible relationships between a casting edge and the surface on which the shadow will fall:
⊥ as in lines AB and DE, or
‖ as in lines BC and CD.

⊥ SHADOWS (ABs and DSE)
- vary dramatically in angle and length
- always begin and end shade/shadow systems
- converge to a separate VP on the VL for the plane in which they lie
- always cut across any rectangular environment at an angle

SUN IN FRONT OF THE VIEWER
- VP for sun's rays is above eyelevel
- most vertical surfaces are in shade with ground shadows in the fore-ground
- usually best for interior perspectives

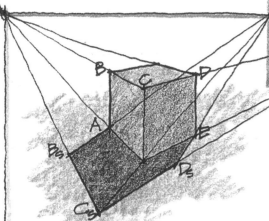

‖ SHADOWS (BsCs and CsDs.)
- are always ‖ to, and the same length as, the line that casts them
- are never connected to the line that casts them
- converge to one of the regular VPs of the perspective framework
- are always ‖ to the edges and joints of the environment

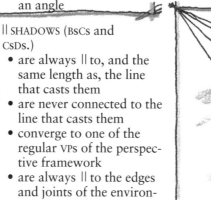

SUN BEHIND THE VIEWER
- VP for sun's rays is below eyelevel
- most vertical surfaces are in sun and shadow, with most ground shadows behind the building
- usually good for exterior perspectives

SHADE/SHADOW SYSTEMS

Most complicated shadow patterns are made up of combinations of three simple shade/shadow systems:

PROJECTED SYSTEMS, in which the shadow pattern is cast by an object projecting from, or appearing to sit on, the shadow-catching surface. In its simplest form this system has at least four casting edges, two of which are ⊥ and two of which are ‖.

INDENTED SYSTEMS, in which the shadow pattern occurs in a recess or indentation in a surface, with the edges of the indentation casting a shadow pattern within the indentation. This system has only two casting edges, each of which casts a shadow that is ⊥ as it angles down the sidewall of the indentation and changes to a ‖ shadow when it hits the bottom.

STEP SYSTEMS, which are the most complex, beginning with ⊥ shadows at each end and alternating relationships from ⊥ to ‖ each time the shadow changes planes.

SHADOW-ANALYSIS CUBE

This cube is made up of three mutually perpendicular planes and three mutually perpendicular struts. The shadow patterns it catches when turned toward the sun represent all the shadow-casting relationships possible in rectangular environments. There are three ⊥ and six ‖ shadow-casting relationships. At any one time, except at coincidence, the sun casts a shadow pattern consisting of three ⊥ shadows and two (of the six possible) ‖ shadows.

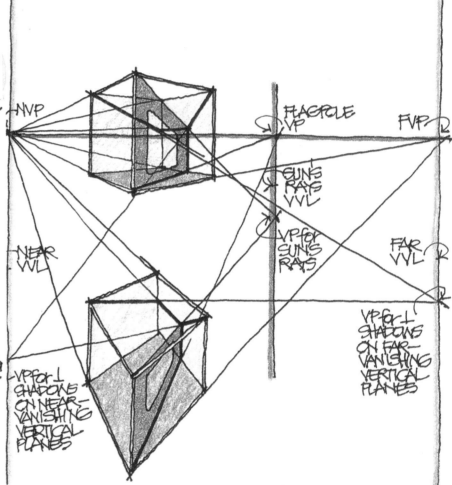

This perspective framework shows the location of all the VPs necessary to cast the shadows in a rectangular environment. As the designer/delineator, you are free to place the sun where it will cast the most characteristic or dramatic shadows, and the best way to do that is to directly choose the angles of two of the three ⊥ shadows. The third ⊥ angle and the VP for the sun's rays are resultants of those first two choices.

83

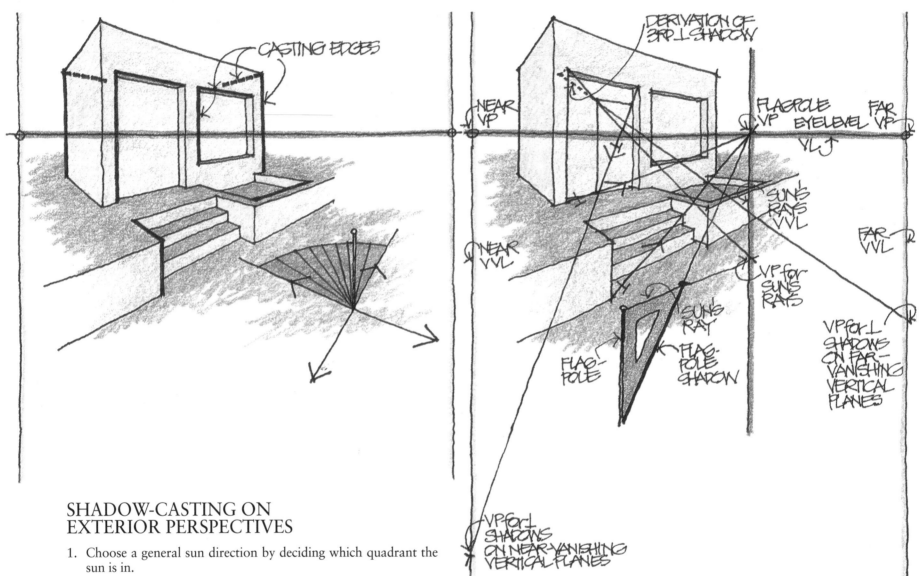

The following labels appear in the illustration:

CASTING EDGES

DERIVATION OF 3RD ⊥ SHADOW

NEAR VP

FLAGPOLE VP   EYELEVEL   FAR VP   VL

FAR VVL

NEAR VVL

NEAR VVL

SUN'S RAYS VVL

VP for SUN'S RAYS

SUN'S RAY

VP for ⊥ SHADOWS ON FAR-VANISHING VERTICAL PLANES

FLAG-POLE

FLAG-POLE SHADOW

VP for ⊥ SHADOWS ON NEAR-VANISHING VERTICAL PLANES

SHADOW-CASTING ON EXTERIOR PERSPECTIVES

1. Choose a general sun direction by deciding which quadrant the sun is in.

2. Make a sun/shade analysis that determines which surfaces are directly facing the sun and which surfaces are turned away from the sun or in shade. The surfaces identified as being in shade should be toned in a light gray because these surfaces will never have sun or shadow on them.

3. Identify the casting edges, which are all the outside corners (including hidden ones) that separate sunlit surfaces from those in shade.

4. Choose the specific sun angle by choosing the angles of two of the three ⊥ shadows.

5. Derive the third ⊥ shadow and establish the VPs for the three ⊥ shadows (on the VLs for the planes in which the shadows lie) as well as the VP for sun's rays (on the vertical vanishing line, or VVL, for the vertical planes of the sun's rays—which is always a vertical line through the flagpole VP). The third ⊥ shadow can often be derived directly in one of the indented shade/shadow systems (as in the doorway recess in the perspective above) or you can draw a shadow-analysis cube in the foreground to verify the derivation. The shadow-analysis cube must be accurate or the shadow angles won't agree.

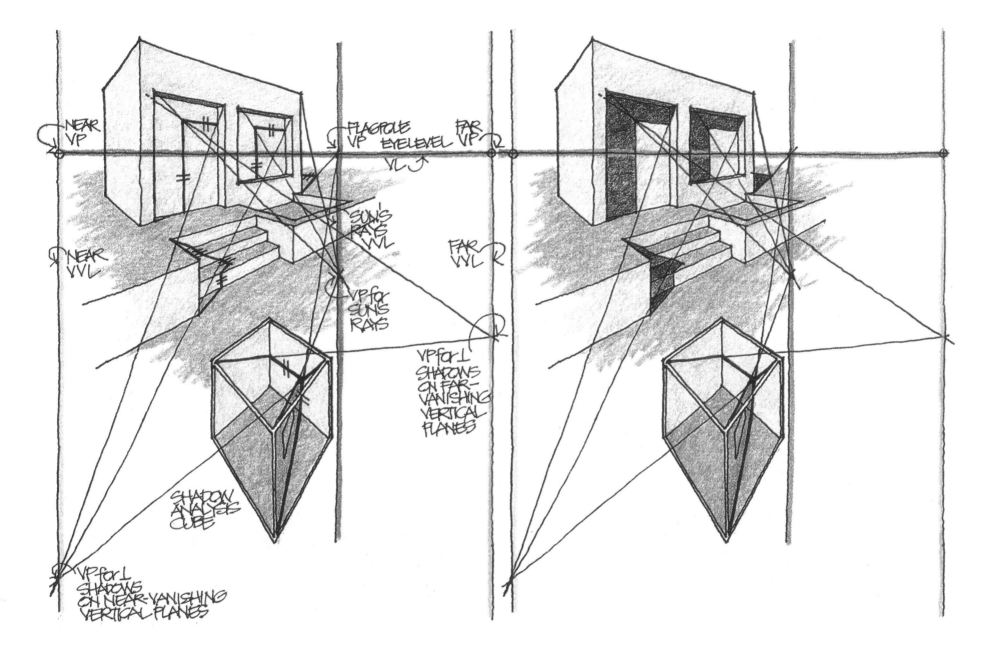

NEAR VP

FLAGPOLE VP

EYELEVEL VL

FAR VP

NEAR VVL

SUN'S RAYS VVL

FAR VVL

VP for SUN'S RAYS

VP for ⊥ SHADOWS ON FAR-VANISHING VERTICAL PLANES

SHADOW ANALYSIS CUBE

VP for ⊥ SHADOWS ON NEAR-VANISHING VERTICAL PLANES

6. Extend all the ⊥ shadows and resolve the shade/shadow systems they initiate with the connecting ∥ shadows.

7. The last step is to render the shadows a darker gray and make sure you understand the shadow-casting perspective framework. After a few times through the procedure you will see that

the resulting shadow pattern can easily be changed and possibly improved by slight changes in the locations of various VPs.

The interesting thing about shadow-casting is that shadow patterns look right when they are correct because we have been reading them all our lives.

SHADOW-CASTING ON INTERIOR PERSPECTIVES

1. Choose a general sun direction by deciding which quadrant the sun is in. Usually it is best to place the sun in front of the viewer so that light and shadow enter the space.

2. Make a sun/shade analysis that determines which surfaces are directly facing the sun, or in sun, and which surfaces are turned away from the sun, or in shade. Surfaces identified as being in shade should be toned light gray because they can have neither sun nor shadows. It is good to tone these shade surfaces right away so the perspective begins to read.

3. Identify the casting edges, which are all the outside corners (including hidden ones) that separate sunlit surfaces from those in shade.

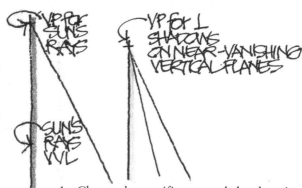

4. Choose the specific sun angle by choosing the angles of two of the three ⊥ shadows. Notice that when the sun is placed in front of the viewer we never see the third ⊥ shadow angle because it can only occur on the vertical sunlit surfaces which are turned away from us. However, we sometimes still need to use its angle, as we will soon see.

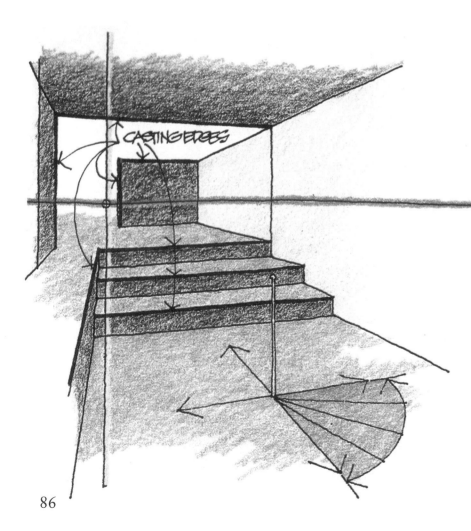

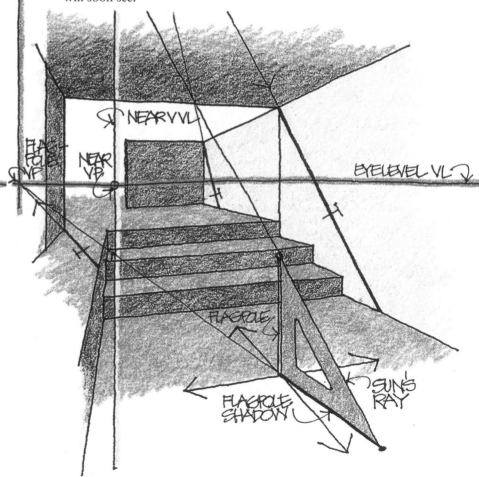

5. Derive the third ⊥ shadow and establish the VPs for the three ⊥ shadows (on the VLs for the planes in which the shadows lie) as well as the VP for sun's rays (on the VVL for the vertical planes of the sun's rays—which is always a vertical line through the flagpole VP). With the sun in front of us, the third ⊥ shadow can only be derived by drawing the shadow-

SUNS RAYS/VVL

analysis cube in the foreground and casting the shadow pattern in it consistent with the two ⊥ shadows already chosen. The shadow-analysis cube must be accurate or the shadow angles won't agree.

6. Extend all the ⊥ shadows and resolve the shade/shadow systems they initiate with the connecting ‖ shadows. The only difficulty in this perspec-

tive is in the lower left corner, where the edge of the upper floor level is casting a ‖ shadow on the three descending steps. This is where the third ⊥ shadow angle is needed to locate the ‖ shadow on each successive step.

The last step is to render the shadows a darker gray and make sure you understand the shadow-casting perspective framework. After a few times through the procedure, you will see that the resulting shadow pattern can easily be changed and possibly improved by slight changes in the locations of various VPs.

The interesting thing about shadow-casting is that shadow patterns look right when they are correct because we have been reading them all our lives.

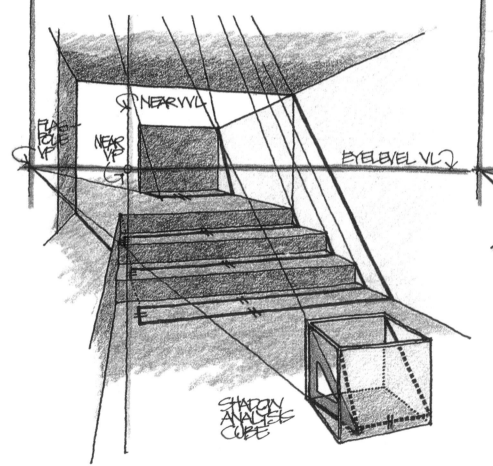

NEAR VVL

FLAG POLE VP

NEAR VP

EYELEVEL VL

SHADOW ANALYSIS CUBE

INDIRECT LIGHT

There are lighting conditions and orientations, like overcast days and north-facing rooms, which completely exclude direct sunlight. There may also be occasions when you just don't have time to cast the shadows. In either case, you should render the space in indirect light.

The first thing to do in rendering an interior in indirect light is to render the contrast between a relatively dark interior and a brightly lighted exterior, seen through the windows. On tracing paper this is most easily done by simply coloring all the openings to the exterior with white Prismacolor on the back and then mounting the tracing on a dark background. Alternatively you may get an underexposed Diazo print on sepia paper or a photocopy on a middletone paper and add Prismacolor non-photo blue and other light colors to the exterior space seen through the windows.

The best way to determine the relative indirect illumination of the six surfaces of any rectangular environment is to place an imaginary cube in the foreground and make some assumptions. The face turned toward the direction of the strongest source of indirect light will have 1 (brightest) and its opposite face will be value 6 (darkest) because it will be most difficult for any light to be reflected 180 degrees backwards to those surfaces. You will have to imagine or assume which surfaces will be next lightest (2) and their parallel partners next darkest (5) and least light (3) and least dark (4). Once these light value assumptions are made, all that remains is to render all surfaces in the environment consistent with this analysis, based on the orientation of each surface.

NIGHT PERSPECTIVES

Many environments we design are used at least as much under artificial illumination as they are in sunlight, yet we seldom study the experience of that nighttime illumination.

The drawing above is a tracing paper sketch mounted on black construction paper. If you need multiple copies or a little slicker presentation you can make color copies of this drawing, mounted on black paper, and reduce or enlarge the drawing in the process. In addition to the original drawing you can also quickly and inexpensively get any perspective sketch you have made photocopied onto a dark paper or, if the drawing is on tracing paper, you can accomplish the same thing by getting an underexposed Diazo print.

You can then simply "turn on the lights" by toning the drawing or print with light Prismacolor pencils on the illuminated interior surfaces and faintly washing light out onto lateral surfaces such as the reveals of openings and the floors of terraces. It is better not to draw light fixtures or light rays. Simply render the illuminated surfaces. The perspective above also uses the analysis described at left under indirect light to render the various surfaces consistently. The surfaces facing us, for instance, would be turned away from any light coming from the shop windows, and darkening them heightens the contrast with the illuminated windows.

In both tracing paper drawings above the rule is to put the white Prismacolor on the back and the black and colors on the front.

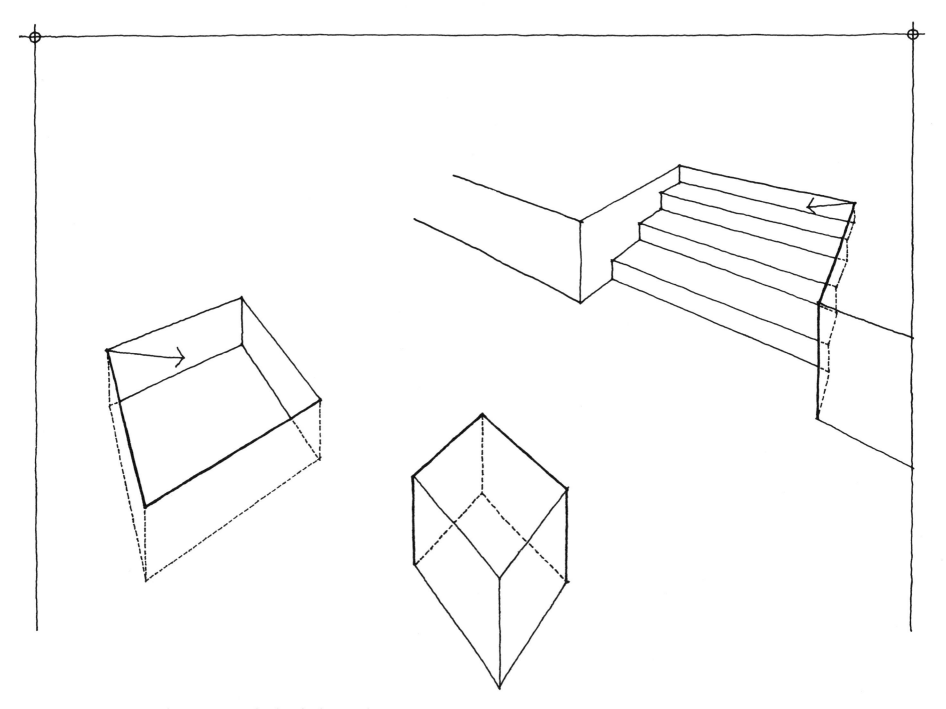

INSTRUCTIONS From the two perpendicular shadow angles given (indicated by arrows) find the flagpole VP, the other two VPs for perpendicular shadows on vertical planes, and the VP for sun's rays. Cast the shadows accordingly. Notice that we are looking at these three shade/shadow systems as if we were the sun. In other words, we won't see any surfaces in shade because they are all turned away from us, and the casting edges are all spatial edges.

89

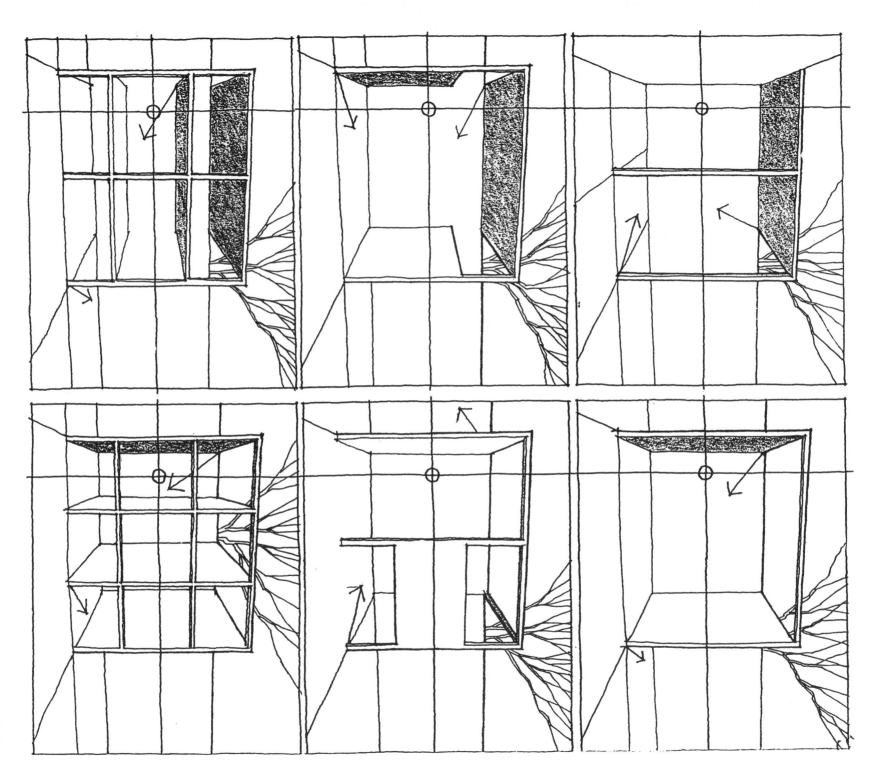

INSTRUCTIONS From the two perpendicular shadow angles given (indicated by arrows) make a sun/shade analysis, identify the casting edges, locate the VPs for the perpendicular shadows, and cast the shadows. Tone the shadows darker than the shade.

90

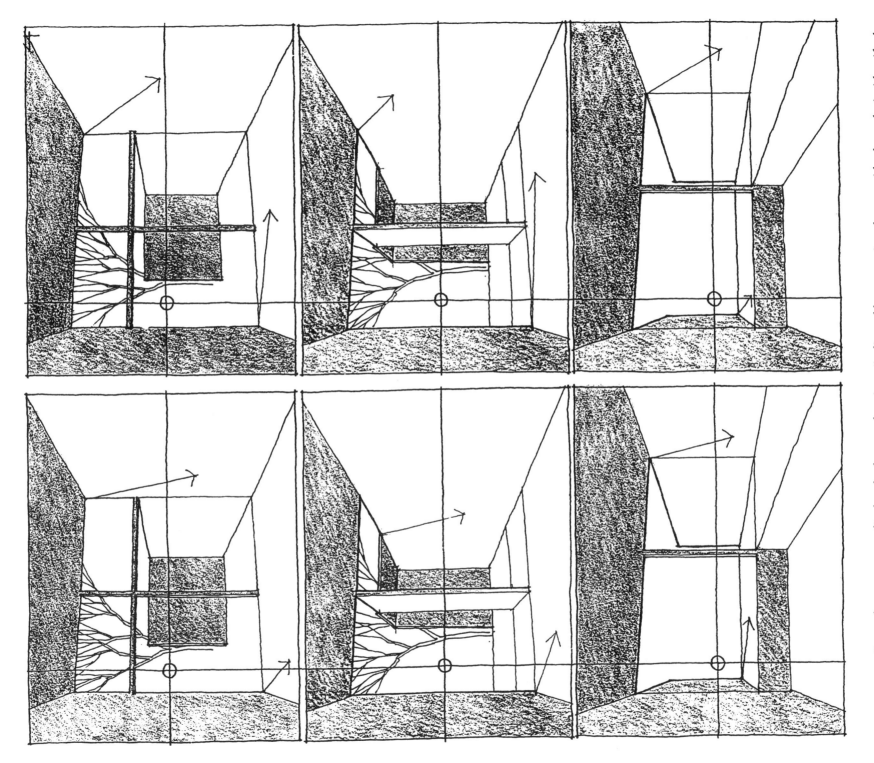

INSTRUCTIONS From the two perpendicular shadow angles given (indicated by arrows) make a sun/shade analysis, identify the casting edges, locate the VPs for the perpendicular shadows, and cast the shadows. Tone the shadows darker than the shade.

91

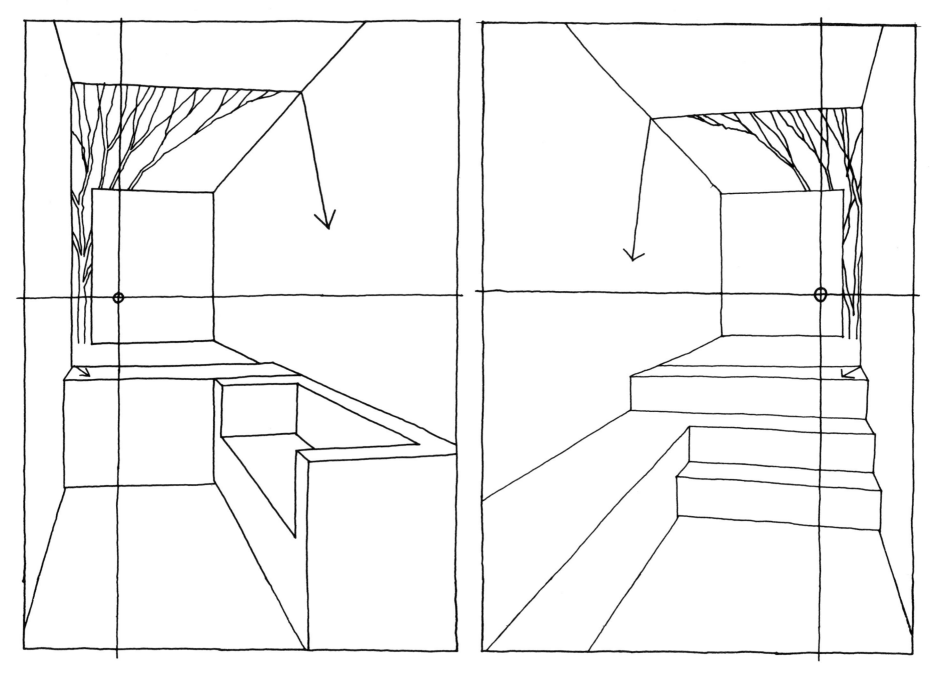

INSTRUCTIONS From the two perpendicular shadow angles given (indicated by arrows) make a sun/shade analysis, tone all the surfaces in shade, identify the casting edges, locate the VPs for the perpendicular shadows, and cast the shadows.

Tone the shadows darker than the shade. Add trees, figure groups, and furniture without obscuring the space or the shadow patterns. Add material textures to the surfaces, beginning with the floor and the most distant vertical surfaces.

92

INSTRUCTIONS From the two perpendicular shadow angles given (indicated by arrows) make a sun/shade analysis, tone all the surfaces in shade, identify the casting edges, locate the VPs for the two perpendicular shadows, and cast the shadows.

Tone the shadows darker than the shade. Add trees, figure groups, and a foreground and background without obscuring the building or the shadow patterns. Add material textures to the surfaces, beginning with the ground plane and the most distant vertical surfaces.

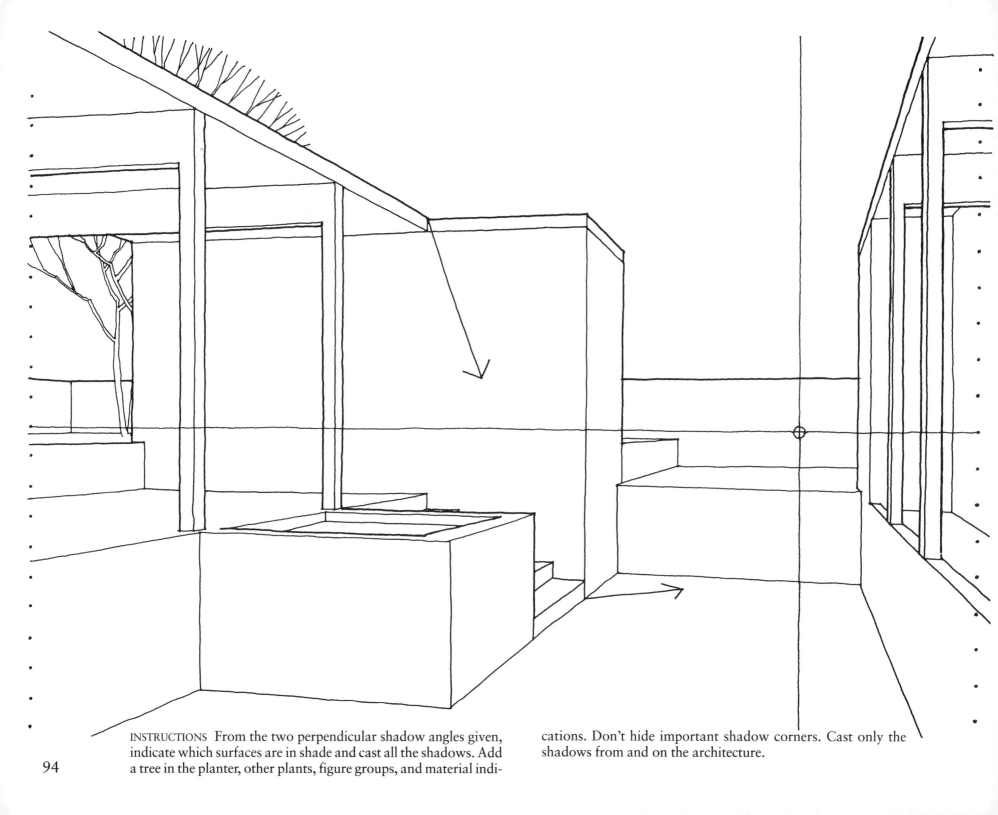

INSTRUCTIONS From the two perpendicular shadow angles given, indicate which surfaces are in shade and cast all the shadows. Add a tree in the planter, other plants, figure groups, and material indi-cations. Don't hide important shadow corners. Cast only the shadows from and on the architecture.

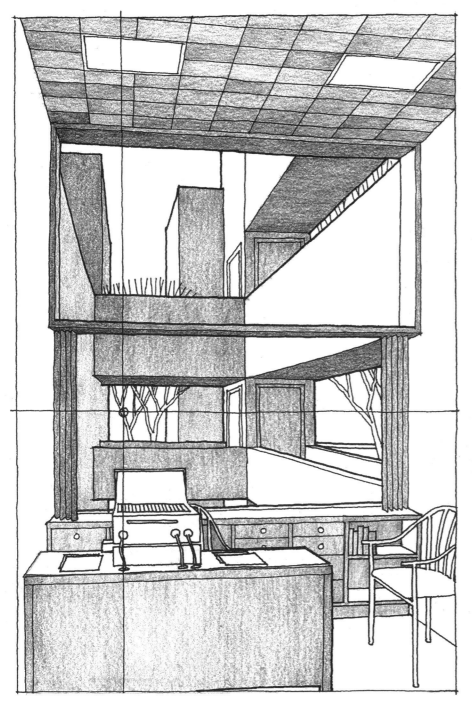

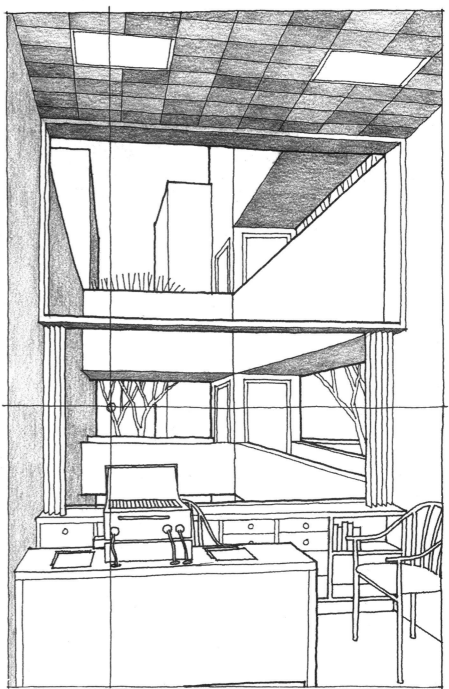

INSTRUCTIONS The sun is in front of us and to our left, putting the toned surfaces in shade. Cast the shadows consistent with this sun location, choosing the angles for the two perpendicular shadows that will make the most interesting drawing.

The sun is behind us and to our left, putting the toned surfaces in shade. Cast the shadows consistent with this sun location, choosing the angles for the two perpendicular shadows that will make the most interesting drawing.

INSTRUCTIONS With pencil tones, render all surfaces (including furniture) as if they were illuminated in indirect light. There will be no shadows. Disregard reflections in the glass. Assume we are facing south on a cloudy afternoon—the light will come from in front of us and from our right. The five visible surface orientations will then be lighted from 1 (lightest) to 5 (darkest) as follows: upward-facing (1), west-facing (2), east-facing (3), down-facing (4), north-facing (5).

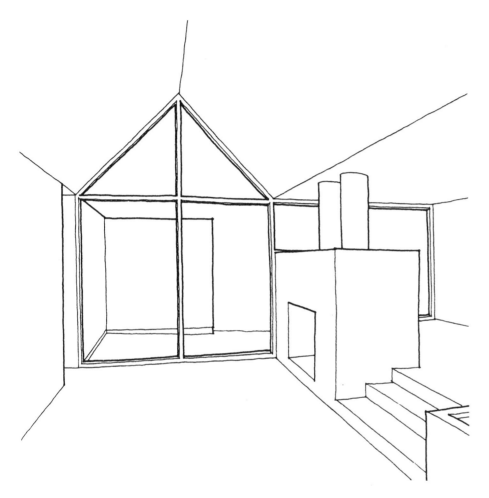

The color coding in this section is a reminder of the first principle of perspective: that the three sets of parallel planes in a perspective converge to three separate VLs.

- Horizontal planes and the horizontal eyelevel VL into which they vanish are colored red.
- Near vanishing vertical planes and the near vertical VL into which they vanish are colored green.
- Far vanishing vertical planes and the far vertical VL into which they vanish are colored blue.

This understanding is necessary in finding VPs for sets of diagonal lines.

8 Spatial Interest: Direct-Perspective Layout

Spatial interest is the basic category of drawing and of environmental interest. Spatial interest in drawings, as in the environment, is a kinesthetic promise—the anticipated experience of watching spaces and vistas that are hidden or partially seen come into view as we move through the spaces. The main sources of spatial interest in drawing are the number and clear representation of these partially revealed objects and spaces. This is done by placing objects in front of surfaces and other objects and profiling the edges that obscure the hidden spaces.

The representation of three-dimensional space in a two-dimensional drawing begins with establishing a measurable spatial structure that will become the environment being designed. In addition to locating the various surfaces and edges of the environment in perspective, such a spatial structure allows the projection and rendering of light in the environment. What is often taught under the separate titles of "perspective" and "shadow-casting" is better understood as part of the same spatial structure.

If environmental designers are to know what the experience of the environments they are designing will be, they must master the drawing of the integrated spatial structure that allows them to represent three-dimensional space in light.

PRINCIPLES

There are only three principles of perspective and they apply to all perspective frameworks and methods.

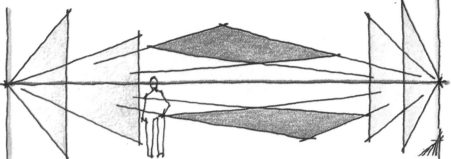

1. Sets of parallel planes converge into VLs at visual infinity.

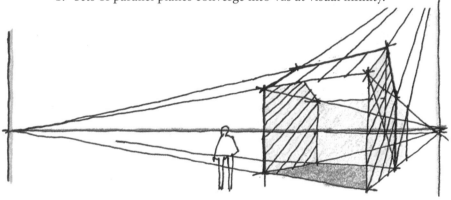

2. Sets of parallel lines converge into VPs on the VL for the plane in which they lie.

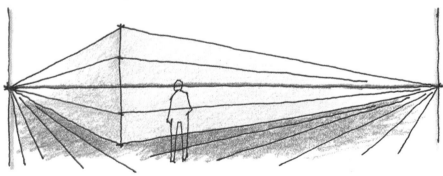

3. VPs for the perspectives of a rectangular object or space are the intersections of the VLs for the horizontal planes and the VLs for the vertical planes.

FRAMEWORKS

Perspective frameworks are arrangements of VLs and VPs based on different assumptions about the viewer's relationship to the object or space being drawn.

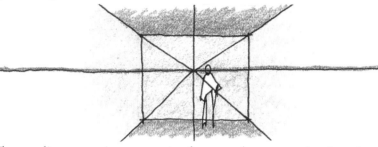

The two-line one-point perspective framework assumes the viewer's line of sight is level and axially aligned with the space or object being drawn.

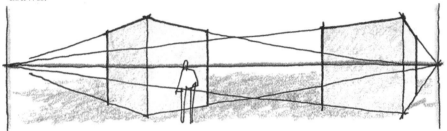

The three-line two-point perspective framework assumes the viewer's line of sight is level but free to turn at any angular relationship to the space or object being drawn.

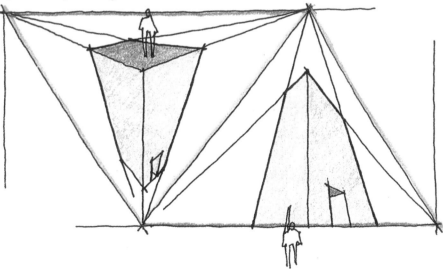

The three-line three-point perspective framework assumes the viewer's line of sight is tipped upward or downward, resulting in a third VP above or below eyelevel.

METHODS

The various perspective methods are all based on the different ways they make the three-dimensional space of the perspective measurable, primarily in the depth dimension.

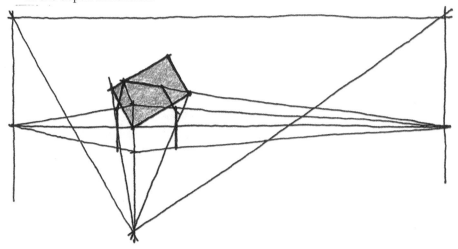

PLAN-PROJECTED METHODS

Conventional perspective methods aspire to an absolute measurability based on laborious drafted projection from a floor plan and section. Projected methods are time-consuming and unpredictable, but their most serious drawback is that they cannot be drawn without a finished plan and section, which dooms them to being tertiary drawings usually completed, if at all, after all design decisions have been made.

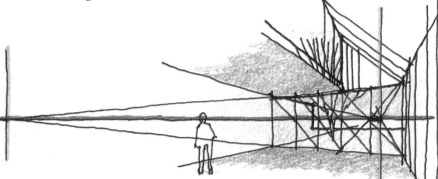

DIRECT-PERSPECTIVE METHOD

The direct-perspective method allows perspectives to be drawn directly, using two vertical planes to measure the width and depth of the space or object to be drawn and requiring only the approximate dimensions and the self-confidence to guess an initial 10' square. Absolute measurability is given up in favor of a relative measurability based on the scale and dimensions of the human figure. This method makes the perspective an equal participant in the design process and allows for study of the experiential quality of the design.

DIAGONALS

Diagonals can be used geometrically to extend or subdivide a rectangular unit. This is best understood on a flat two-dimensional surface.

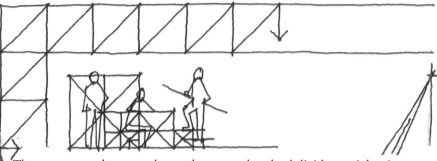

The same procedures can be used to extend and subdivide spatial units on the flat surfaces of any space or object drawn in perspective. Subdivision by diagonals can be understood at a glance, but there are two ways of using diagonals for extension:

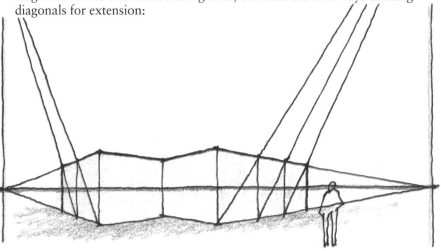

1. By finding a VP for diagonals. Use the second principle of perspective to establish a VP for each parallel set of diagonals on the VL for the plane in which they lie.

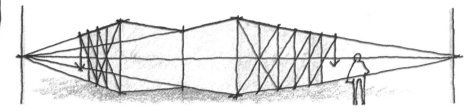

2. By using diagonals through the bisectors of successive 10' spatial units. Use 5' increments so that all spatial units remain square and all diagonals are 45 degrees.

99

WIDTH PLANE

The width plane is a vertical plane placed across the object or space to be drawn. It is a convenient way of measuring the widths and heights needed to draw a perspective. The plane should be placed at the most convenient measuring position—usually across the most interesting wall of an interior space or the most interesting facade of a building or object.

DEPTH PLANE

The depth plane is a vertical plane placed along the side of the building or space to be drawn. It is a convenient way of measuring the depths and heights needed to draw a perspective. The plane should be placed along the most distant side wall, because the initial depth estimation, on which all successive spatial extensions will be based, is much more accurate if the most distant side wall is used.

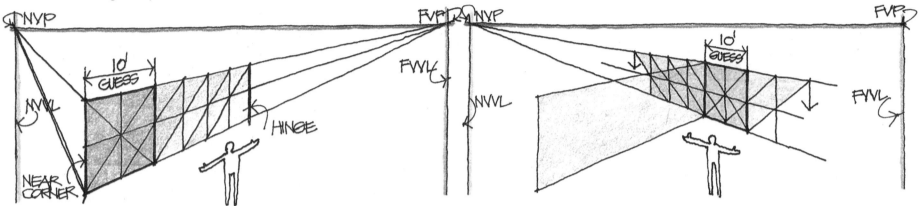

The measuring is done by first guessing a 10' square in the plane and then extending and subdividing the space along the width plane using diagonals, either extended from a VP for diagonals on the far vertical (blue) VL or by using successive diagonals through the squares' bisectors.

The measuring is done by first guessing a 10' square standing in the plane and then extending and subdividing the space along the depth plane using diagonals, either extended from a VP for diagonals on the near vertical (green) VL or by using successive diagonals through the squares' bisectors.

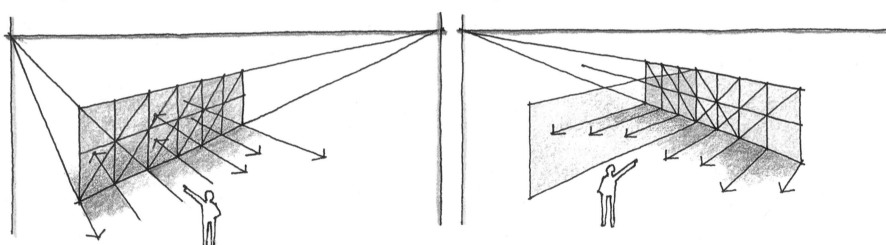

Widths needed in front of or behind the width plane must also be measured off on the width plane and then pulled forward from, or pushed backward toward, the near VP (arrows).

Depths needed at other places in the perspective must all be measured off along the depth plane and then pulled out into the space or object from the far VP (arrows).

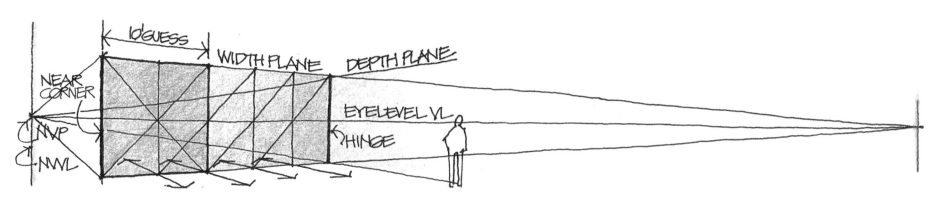

LAYING OUT AN EXTERIOR PERSPECTIVE

1. Draw a horizontal eyelevel line. **2.** Place a VP at each end of the eyelevel line as far apart as possible. **3.** Choose the building's most interesting face and side, placing the corner that is their intersection (the near corner) so the face extends transversely across the drawing toward the far VP. **4.** Extend the near corner an equal distance above and below the eyelevel line. (If we assume that the eyelevel line is at about 5', then the near corner we have just drawn is about 10' tall.) **5.** Draw lines from the top and bottom of the near corner to the two VPs, forming two intersecting vertical planes 10' tall. (The longer of these two planes, extending transversely across the drawing from the near corner toward the far VP, is called the width plane and is colored blue because it converges into the blue far VVL.) **6.** Guess a 10' square standing in the width plane beginning at the near corner and extending toward the far VP.

7. The width of the building's face and all the necessary points within it (windows and doors) can now be measured off by using diagonals. Other width dimensions needed elsewhere in the perspective also have to be measured here and then pulled toward or away from the near VP to wherever they are needed in the perspective (arrows). **8.** Continue measuring along the width plane to the distant corner of the face of the building. This vertical line is called the hinge because this is where the green depth plane (green because it vanishes into the green near VVL) is hinged at 90 degrees to the blue width plane by drawing lines from the top and bottom of the hinge to the near VP (continued on p. 102).

LAYING OUT AN INTERIOR PERSPECTIVE

1. Draw a horizontal eyelevel line. **2.** Choose the space's most interesting end wall and side wall and place the corner that is their intersection (the near corner) so the end walls extend transversely across the drawing toward the far VP. **3.** Having placed the near corner strongly on one side of the drawing, extend it an equal distance above and below the eyelevel line. (If we assume that the eyelevel line is at about 5', then the near corner we have just drawn is about 10' tall.) **4.** Draw lines from the top and bottom of the near corner across the drawing, converging slightly and equally to a far VP (perhaps too distant to reach) and forming two intersecting vertical planes 10' tall. (The longer of these two planes, extending transversely across the drawing from the near corner toward the far VP, is called the width plane and is colored blue because it converges into the blue far VVL.) **5.** Guess a 10' square standing in the width plane beginning at the near corner and extending toward the far VP. **6.** Choose a near VP within the first 10' square, no more than 5' from the near corner.

7. The width of the end wall and all the necessary points within it (windows and doors) can now be measured off by using diagonals. Other width dimensions needed elsewhere in the perspective also have to be measured here and then pulled toward or away from the near VP to wherever they are needed in the perspective (arrows). **8.** Continue measuring along the width plane to the distant narrow end of the end wall of the space. This vertical corner is called the hinge because this is where the green depth plane (green because it vanishes into the green near VVL) is hinged at 90 degrees to the blue width plane by drawing lines from the top and bottom of the hinge to the near VP (continued on p. 102).

101

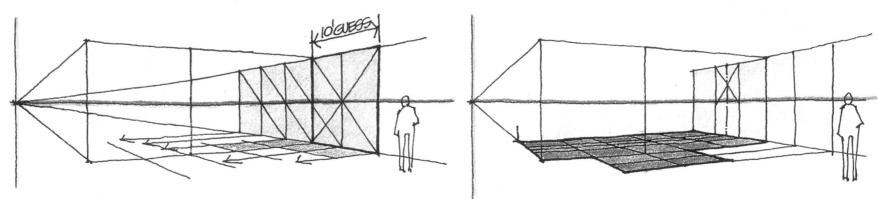

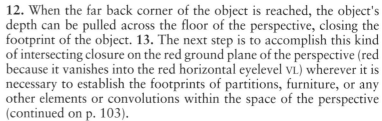

9. Next, guess a 10' square standing in the green depth plane and extending in front of the hinge. **10.** Once this square is guessed, all the depths necessary to draw the perspective are measured off along the depth plane by extending one of the diagonals of the 10' square to intersect the near VVL, establishing a VP for diagonals. Successive spatial units can now be marked off by diagonals from this VP. If such a VP for diagonals is inconvenient to reach, the same measuring is accomplished by using diagonals through the bisectors of successive squares. **11.** The depths thus measured will have to be pulled across the perspective from the far VP to wherever they are needed (arrows).

12. When the far back corner of the object is reached, the object's depth can be pulled across the floor of the perspective, closing the footprint of the object. **13.** The next step is to accomplish this kind of intersecting closure on the red ground plane of the perspective (red because it vanishes into the red horizontal eyelevel VL) wherever it is necessary to establish the footprints of partitions, furniture, or any other elements or convolutions within the space of the perspective (continued on p. 103).

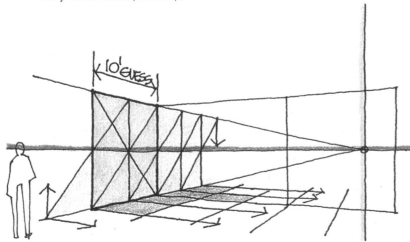

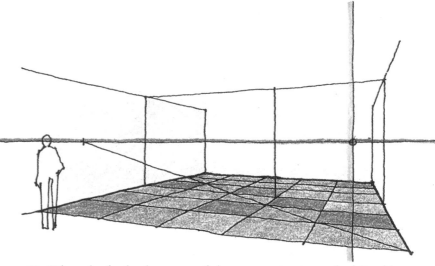

9. Next, guess a 10' square standing in the green depth plane and extending in front of the hinge. **10.** Once this square is guessed, all the depths necessary to draw the perspective are measured off along the depth plane by extending one of the diagonals of the 10' square to intersect the near VVL, establishing a VP for diagonals. Successive spatial units can now be marked off by diagonals from this VP. If such a VP for diagonals is inconvenient to reach, the same measuring is accomplished by using diagonals through the bisectors of successive squares. **11.** The depths thus measured will have to be pulled across the perspective from the far VP to wherever they are needed (arrows).

12. When the far back corner of the perspective is reached (in this case a patio extending beyond the glass back wall), the space's depth can be pulled across the floor of the perspective, closing the footprint of the space. **13.** The next step is to accomplish this kind of intersecting closure on the red floor plane of the perspective (red because it vanishes into the red horizontal eyelevel VL) wherever it is necessary to establish the footprints of the partitions, furniture, or any other elements or convolutions within the space of the perspective (continued on p. 103).

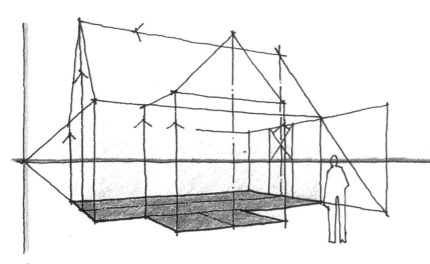

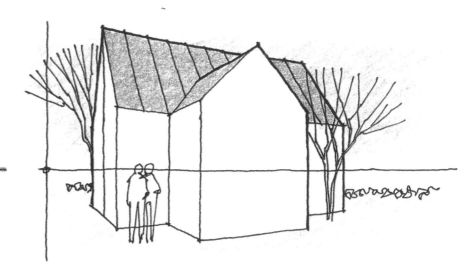

14. Next, the corners of the various footprints are pulled up vertically to their full heights. A vertical dimension is easily determined anywhere in the perspective because the measurement from any point on the floor to the eyelevel VL is always 5'. That distance is easily subdivided or extended to the height needed.

It is important to realize that these perspectives are drawn directly without a drafted plan, elevation, or section, and without an architectural scale. Rather, we relied completely on the 5' height of the human eye level as the basis for all our measurements.

If the resulting perspective is not the view anticipated, we can just as quickly draw another view or change the viewer's eye level or the size of the drawing, as shown on the next page. Most importantly, we have seen the space in three dimensions, as it will actually be experienced, and it is most likely that this visualization will provoke improvements in the design. Drawing perspectives directly and early in the design process can help you discover a need for improvement and provide you with the opportunity to accomplish it.

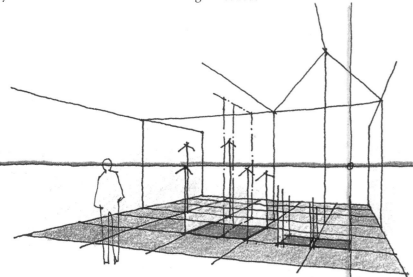

14. Next, the corners of the various footprints are pulled up vertically to their full heights. A vertical dimension is easily determined anywhere in the perspective because the measurement from any point on the floor to the eyelevel VL is always 5'. That distance is easily subdivided or extended to the height needed.

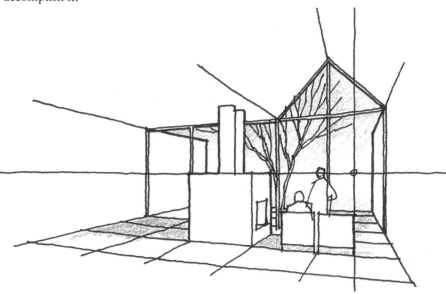

CHANGING VERTICAL POSITION AND SIZE

One of the advantages of the direct perspective method is that vertical and horizontal relationships to the viewer are directly adjustable as the drawing develops, without the repositioning and reprojection necessary with plan-projected methods. This flexibility allows both the vertical position and the size of the drawing to be easily adjusted.

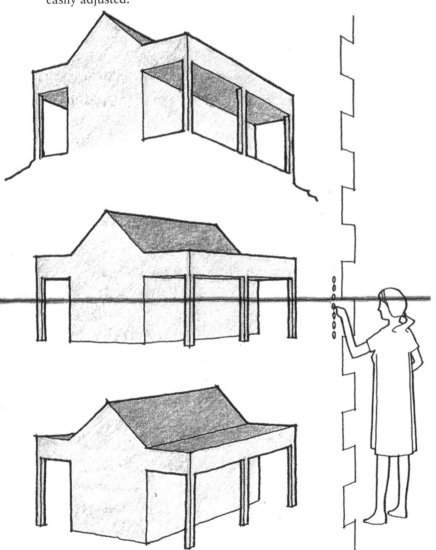

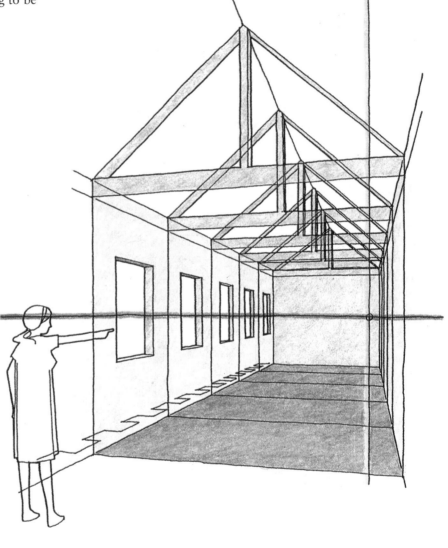

THE ELEVATOR SHAFT:
VERTICAL ADJUSTMENT OF DIRECT PERSPECTIVES
The object or environment can be raised or lowered in relation to the viewer and the viewer's eyelevel as if it were an elevator cab moving up or down a vertical shaft. You can select the level you wish by deciding that the floor level be a specific dimension above or below your eyelevel. Remember that the eyelevel remains a horizontal plane through the viewer's eyes.

THE TUNNEL:
SIZE OR DEPTH ADJUSTMENT OF DIRECT PERSPECTIVES
The size of a direct perspective is adjusted by moving the width plane or the primary face of an object or space backward or forward, toward or from the near VP, along the tunnel of the perspective framework.

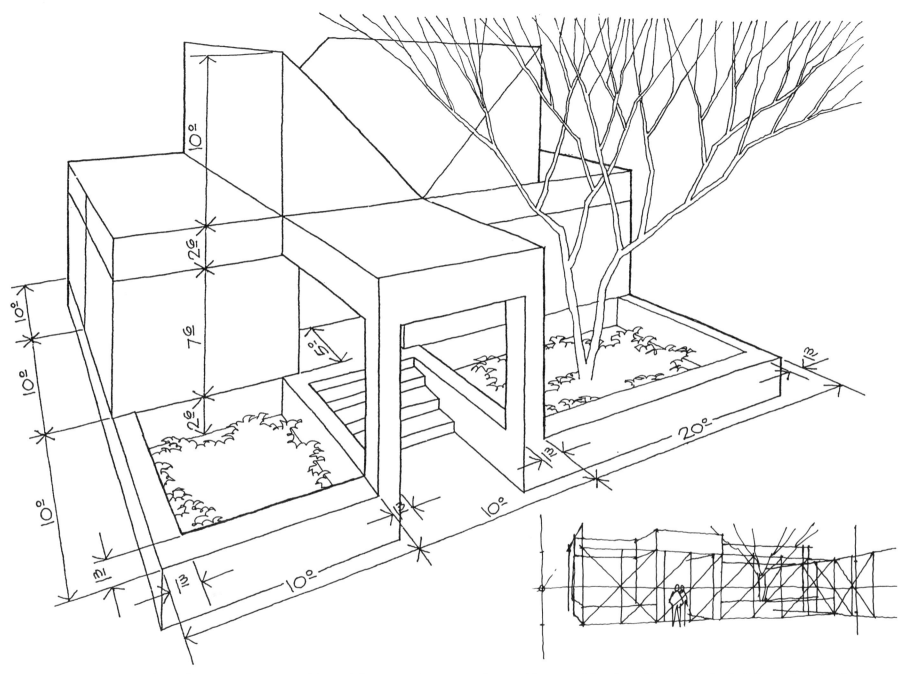

INSTRUCTIONS From the information given in this aerial perspective, draw an eyelevel perspective of the building viewed from the same plan angle as the aerial perspective. On an 8 1/2" x 11" sheet of paper establish a width plane by drawing two vertical scales 10 1/2" apart with the left scale at 1/4" and the right scale at 3/16". Assume the width plane to be on the front face of the projecting portico. Eyelevel should be 5' above the outside ground level, or 30" above the building's floor level. Set the near (left) corner of the building 1 1/4" in from the left vertical scale. Measure 10' squares across the front of the building and hinge on the depth plane running along the far right end of the building (see inset drawing to understand setup). Cast the shadows, select materials, and add landscaping and figures.

105

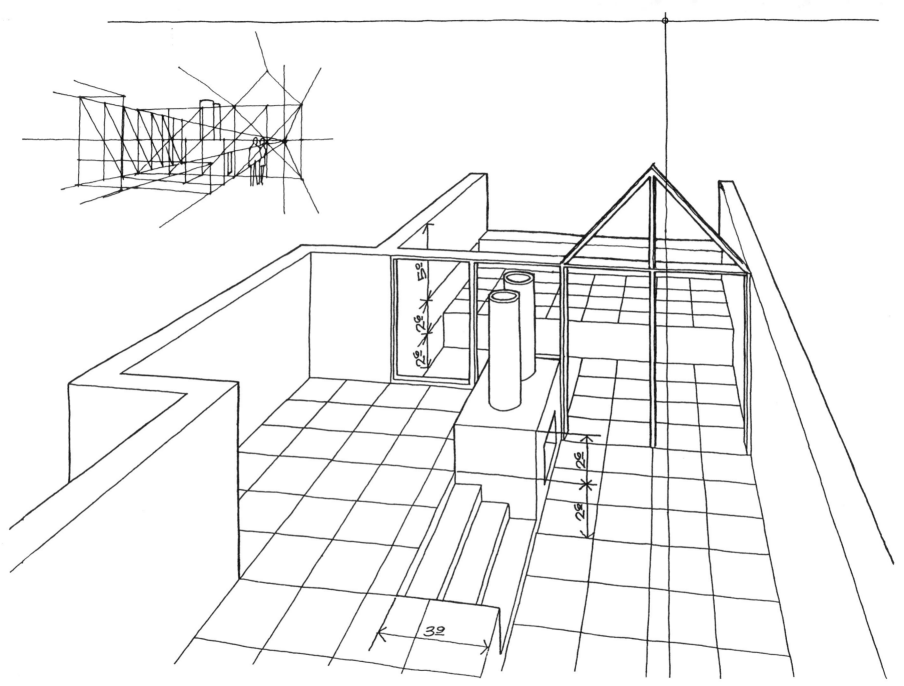

INSTRUCTIONS From the information given in the aerial perspective above, draw an eyelevel perspective of the interior viewed from the right-hand side of the space, looking in the same direction as the aerial. Establish the width plane across the window wall by drawing two vertical scales 10 1/2" on an 8 1/2" x 11" sheet of paper, with the left scale at 1/4" and the right scale at 3/8". Set the near (right) corner of the building 1" in from the right vertical scale. Measure 10' squares across the front of the room and hinge on the depth plane running along the far left wall of the room (see inset drawing to understand setup). Cast the shadows, select materials, and add landscaping and figures. See example perspective of a similar space on pages 101–103.

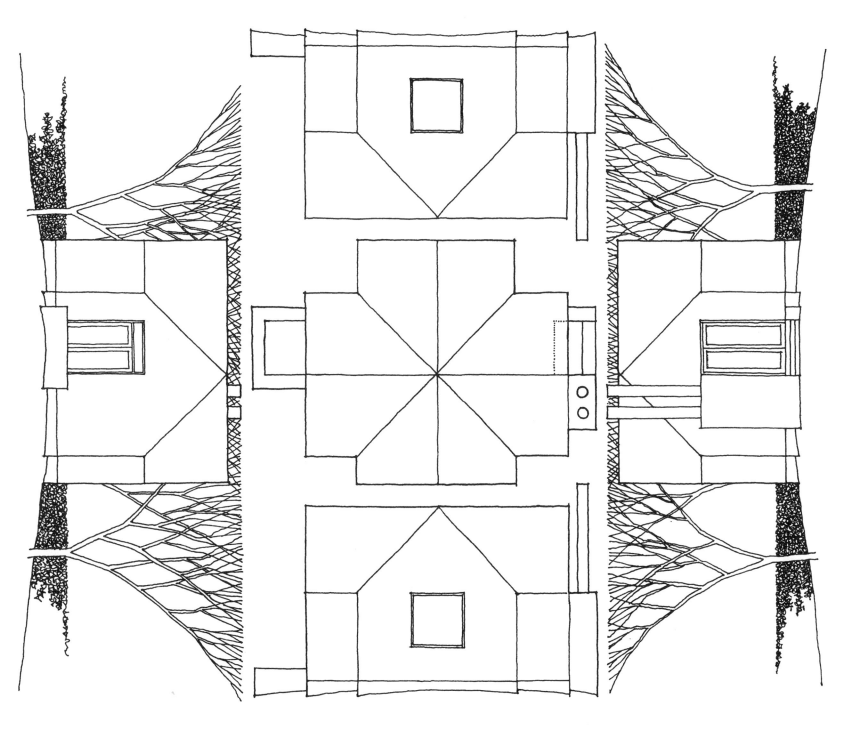

INSTRUCTIONS Draw an eyelevel perspective of the building described in the 1/8" plan and elevations above. Establish the width plane across the front wall by drawing two vertical scales 10 1/2" apart with the left scale at 1/4" and the right scale at 3/8". Set up the two vertical scales 10 1/2" apart on an 8 1/2" x 11" sheet of paper. Set the near (right) corner of the building 3 1/2" in from the right vertical scale. Measure 10' squares across the front of the building and hinge on the depth plane running along the far left wall. Based on the ground sloping away from the building, assume that eyelevel is only 30" above floor level. Cast the shadows, select materials, and add landscaping and figures.

107

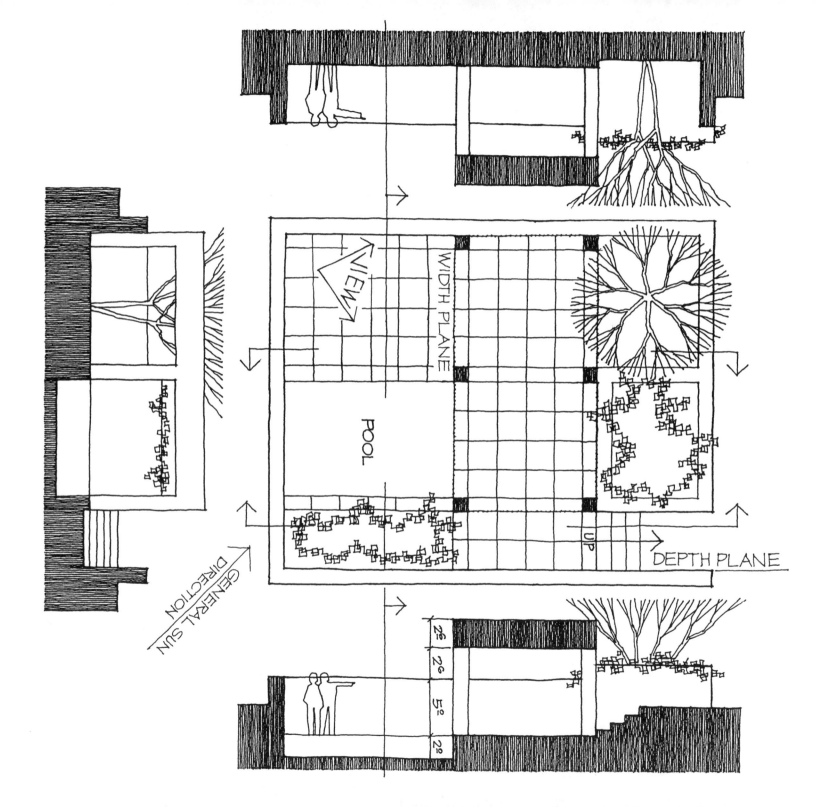

INSTRUCTIONS Draw an eyelevel perspective of the ramada shown in the 1/8" plan and sections above, viewed from the left side. The floor grid is 30", the columns are 15" square, the stair risers are 7 1/2", and the treads 15". Establish the width plane shown in the plan by drawing two vertical scales 10 1/2" apart on an 8 1/2" x 11" sheet of paper, with the right vertical scale at 1/4" and the left scale at 3/8". Set the near (right) corner of the ramada 1" in from the left vertical scale. Measure 10' squares across the width plane to the hinge and then turn the depth plane along the far right wall. Choose a specific sun angle consistent with the width plane to the hinge and then turn the depth plane along the far right wall. Choose a specific sun angle consistent with the general sun direction shown in the plan, cast the shadows, and add materials, figures, and landscaping.

108

POOL

WIDTH PLANE

VIEW

DEPTH PLANE

UP

GENERAL SUN DIRECTION

2⁶

2⁶

5⁰

2⁰

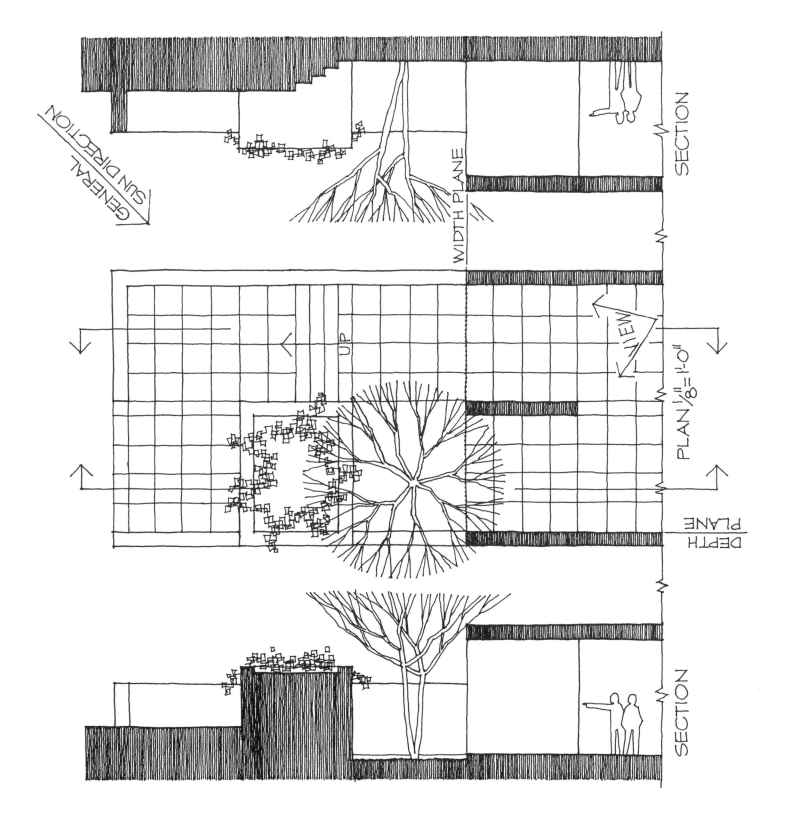

GENERAL SUN DIRECTION

SECTION

WIDTH PLANE

PLAN ⅛" = 1'-0"

VIEW

UP

DEPTH PLANE

SECTION

INSTRUCTIONS Draw an eyelevel perspective of the space shown in the ⅛" plan and sections above, viewed from the right side. The floor grid is 30", the walls are 15" thick, the stair risers are 7½", and the treads 15". Establish the width plane shown in the section by drawing two vertical scales 10½" apart on an 8½" × 11" sheet of paper, with the left scale at ¼" and the right scale at ⅜". Set the near (right) corner of the space 1" in from the right vertical scale. Measure 10' squares across the width plane to the hinge and then turn the depth plane along the far left wall. Choose a specific sun angle consistent with the general sun direction shown in the plan, cast the shadows, and add materials, figures, and landscaping. A common mistake is to guess the first 10' square in the depth plane too deep.

109

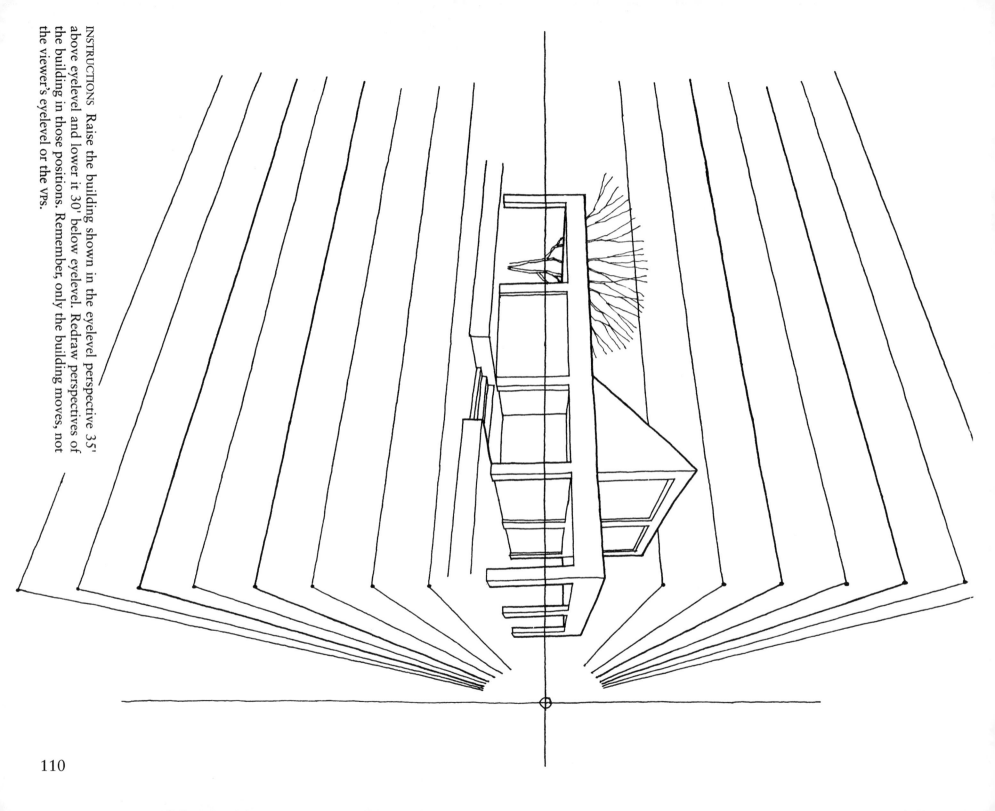

INSTRUCTIONS Raise the building shown in the eyelevel perspective 35' above eyelevel and lower it 30' below eyelevel. Redraw perspectives of the building in those positions. Remember, only the building moves, not the viewer's eyelevel or the VPs.

⑨ Drawing Smart

Although learning that drawing is an enjoyable, satisfying experience is one of the goals of this book, as a professional designer you will be under constant pressure to produce drawings quickly to meet necessary deadlines, and few clients will be interested in paying you to make elaborate, time-consuming drawings. The trick is to learn to make impressive drawings quickly and never let your clients learn how little time they actually take.

There are at least three ways to improve your efficiency as a delineator. Two of them involve self-management and the third is based on using available reprographics techniques as shortcuts.

The first self-management technique is to understand and master line-and-tone drawing and use it to add interest categories in sequential stages. Thus, you only add time-consuming tones and textures if you have determined you have time and if the drawing is worth that investment.

The second self-management technique is to use tracing paper overlays to refine the drawing from a rough sketch to a finished drawing. Learn to make intermediate layers of drawings between a rough sketch and a finished, highly resolved drawing, and you will save time. Rough, sketchy, colored perspectives made as tracing paper overlays of the first perspective layouts can have great life and character and are perfectly acceptable as presentation drawings.

The last great time-saver is employing reproduction techniques. Line drawings can be turned into line-and-tone-on-middletone drawings by using underexposed Diazo prints or photocopies on colored paper. The technique gives you a middletone background color instantly and can result in striking, efficient renderings.

Self-management techniques and reproduction shortcuts will never draw for you or make up for your not learning to draw. They are only benefits for those who have mastered the basic design-drawing skills.

LINE-AND-TONE'S INVESTMENT HIERARCHY

One of the unique advantages of the line-and-tone technique is its open-endedness. Line-and-tone drawings can be made in stages that produce an acceptable drawing quickly and then allow you to add detail in whatever time you have left. This is analogous to the way journalists are taught to write news articles: they get all the important facts covered in the first paragraph and then add further detail in a descending order of importance, because they know that the whole story may run if it's a slow news day but may not if there are more important events.

Like the newspaper story, beyond the first stage the drawing will never look unfinished (as other techniques may) and you can return to the drawing and improve it when you have time. This investment hierarchy is best understood in terms of the drawing interest categories: spatial, tonal, textural, and additional.

When a rough design sketch is selected to be made into a more finished drawing, it should first be given an accurate framework—either drafted, like the one at right, or drawn freehand, if your freehand skill is well developed. This underlying spatial structure is always the first investment on which everything else will stand. If it is made accurately, it is a solid investment in the future of the drawing, which will never have to be made again. You may revise the drawing many times to accommodate design changes or make it suitable for publication by raising its formality. If the initial layout is inaccurate or distorted, however, you will need to start over, which means you wasted time in making the faulty framework.

This framework should also include possible shadow patterns, material selections, and the placement of figures, furniture, and trees so they, along with everything else, will have the benefit of refinement. Sometimes procrastination can be of great benefit to a designer, but drawing procrastination—caused by a fear of being unable to cast shadows or draw decent entourage—can be deadly. If you have a habit of putting off drawing those elements, break that habit.

The spatially profiled open-line drawing at right is an example of the first stage of a line-and-tone drawing. It is very much like the simple line drawings in a child's coloring book, but everything is spatially defined and it is a very committed, unequivocal drawing. Spatial interest consists entirely of partially hidden spaces that invite the observer to become a participant in exploring the space. These partially hidden spaces perform a spatial striptease by promising, "Come over here and I'll show you something you can't see from where you are." It is this promise that makes environments spatially interesting.

The intelligent integration of additional interest can greatly help to demonstrate the spatial interest an environment may have. The placement of figures, furniture, trees, and landscaping automatically specifies the scale and can also indicate what kind of space the drawing is trying to represent. Most importantly, however, these elements of additional interest in distant spaces and on upper and lower levels can demonstrate the configuration of the space and the rewards of exploring it.

Spatial interest and items of additional interest should be tightly interrelated. The number of hidden spaces and spatial layers or laps should be maximized and objects of additional interest should demonstrate the space without hiding space-defining intersections, like the tree outside and the figure on the mezzanine do. The drawing communicates the environment but stops short of having tonal or textural interest, which are the two most time-consuming interest categories to apply. Still, it doesn't appear unfinished or incomplete.

What has been drawn is also a sound investment in the hierarchy because it is an accurate perspective framework with integrated objects of additional interest. If there is a need or opportunity to return to the drawing, this solid initial investment will support added tone and texture.

SPATIAL AND ADDITIONAL INTEREST

The spatially profiled open-line drawing at right is an example of the first stage of a line-and-tone drawing. It is very much like the simple line drawings in a child's coloring book, but everything is spatially defined and it is a very committed, unequivocal drawing.

Spatial interest consists entirely of partially hidden spaces that invite the observer to become a participant in exploring the space. These partially hidden spaces perform a spatial striptease by promising, "Come over here and I'll show you something you can't see from where you are." It is this promise that makes environments spatially interesting.

The intelligent integration of additional interest can greatly help to demonstrate the spatial interest an environment may have. The placement of figures, furniture, trees, and landscaping automatically specifies the scale and can also indicate what kind of space the drawing is trying to represent. Most importantly, however, these elements of additional interest in distant spaces and on upper and lower levels can demonstrate the configuration of the space and the rewards of exploring it.

Spatial interest and items of additional interest should be tightly interrelated. The number of hidden spaces and spatial layers or laps should be maximized and objects of additional interest should demonstrate the space without hiding space-defining intersections, like the tree outside and the figure on the mezzanine do. The drawing communicates the environment but stops short of having tonal or textural interest, which are the two most time-consuming interest categories to apply. Still, it doesn't appear unfinished or incomplete.

What has been drawn is also a sound investment in the hierarchy because it is an accurate perspective framework with integrated objects of additional interest. If there is a need or opportunity to return to the drawing, this solid initial investment will support added tone and texture.

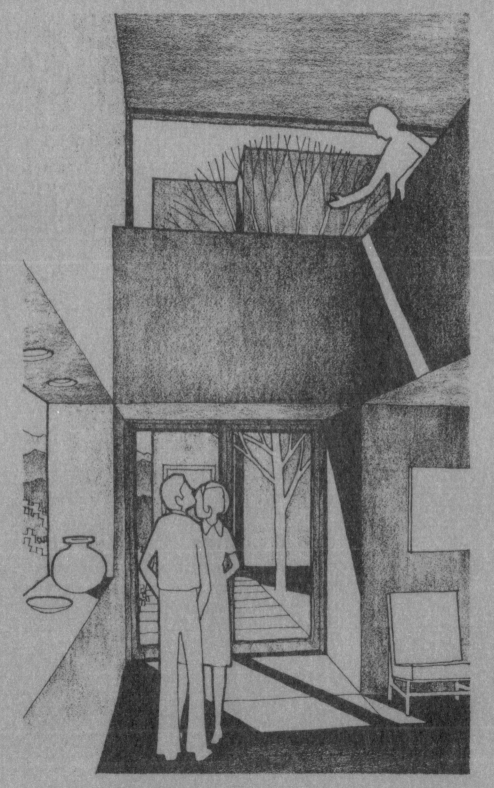

TONAL INTEREST

The two remaining interest categories are both very time-consuming. Tonal interest should be applied next because its main source, light, is not as arbitrary as the main source of textural interest, materials, and because tonal interest lends itself to various technological shortcuts, discussed on page 128.

In the line-and-tone technique, the tones, including colored tones, should be smooth, flat, and characterless. Don't draw or render wood grain, leaf textures, or masonry units with the pencil. All textural rendering should be done with pen. This will preserve the distinction between edge-indicating lines drawn with a pen and surface-indicating tones drawn with a pencil or marker.

The strongest way to indicate tones is to cast the shadows from direct sunlight, letting the sun come into the spaces, with shadows falling over the walls and floors of the space in the most revealing way. The projection of the shadows takes a little time to learn, but it is worth the effort. Arbitrary toning always looks bogus, but toning a space according to sunlight, shade, and shadow gives your drawing the appearance of reality.

The sun angle, which produces the pattern of tonal interest, is a matter of choice. It deserves careful study because it should be tightly integrated with figures and other entourage. Just as they should never hide the space-defining intersections of the architecture, elements of additional interest, like trees and figures, should never hide important shadows, especially those of corners, those that break over steps, and those produced by recesses or projections of the architecture.

TONAL INTEREST

The two remaining interest categories are both very time-consuming. Tonal interest should be applied next because its main source, light, is not as arbitrary as the main source of textural interest, materials, and because tonal interest lends itself to various technological shortcuts, discussed on page 128.

In the line-and-tone technique, the tones, including colored tones, should be smooth, flat, and characterless. Don't draw or render wood grain, leaf textures, or masonry units with the pencil. All textural rendering should be done with pen. This will preserve the distinction between edge-indicating lines drawn with a pen and surface-indicating tones drawn with a pencil or marker.

The strongest way to indicate tones is to cast the shadows from direct sunlight, letting the sun come into the spaces, with shadows falling over the walls and floors of the space in the most revealing way. The projection of the shadows takes a little time to learn, but it is worth the effort. Arbitrary toning always looks bogus, but toning a space according to sunlight, shade, and shadow gives your drawing the appearance of reality.

The sun angle, which produces the pattern of tonal interest, is a matter of choice. It deserves careful study because it should be tightly integrated with figures and other entourage. Just as they should never hide the space-defining intersections of the architecture, elements of additional interest, like trees and figures, should never hide important shadows, especially those of corners, those that break over steps, and those produced by recesses or projections of the architecture.

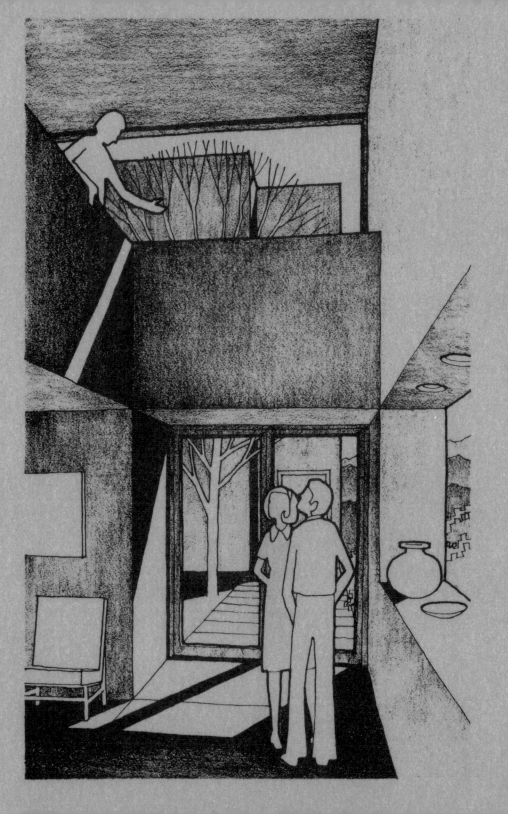

116

TEXTURAL INTEREST

In the hierarchy suggested here, textural interest is the last category to be added. This is because the addition of textural interest is very time-consuming and, unlike tonal interest, it doesn't lend itself to technological shortcuts. It also tends to be the interest category most subject to change, since its main source, materials, is often considered late in the design decision-making process and frequently is adjusted to the construction budget.

In line-and-tone drawings, textural interest should be applied only with pen and applied first to the space-defining surfaces, beginning with the floor or ground plane. These surfaces should always be rendered continuously because intermittent texturing destroys the perception of the surface as a continuous background. Objects standing in front of these textured surfaces should never be textured; rather, they should remain open silhouettes so the viewer's perception continues past them to the textured surface beyond. The choice of how to render textures is always a critical decision and should be based on the most difficult place you will have to draw the texture. If the material is limited in area and in the foreground, like the floor tile in the perspective at right, you can draw it with a double-line joint with great effect and without spending a great deal of time. If the same tile had been extended outside on the walk leading to the distant building, such an indication wouldn't work. It would have been physically impossible to draw it beyond the doorway.

The indication of materials in a design drawing is crucial to an understanding of what the environment will be like when built. Textural interest is the most intimate of the interest categories because it cues remembered tactile experiences. The drawing of a brick floor triggers our remembrance of what it feels like to walk barefoot across a cool brick floor on a hot summer day.

Being able to draw a broad range of materials is important for a designer because as long as we make our own design drawings, we probably won't work with materials we can't draw success-fully. Therefore, we need to draw them all, or at least the ones we prefer.

TEXTURAL INTEREST

In the hierarchy suggested here, textural interest is the last category to be added. This is because the addition of textural interest is very time-consuming and, unlike tonal interest, it doesn't lend itself to technological shortcuts. It also tends to be the interest category most subject to change, since its main source, materials, is often considered late in the design decision-making process and frequently is adjusted to the construction budget.

In line-and-tone drawings, textural interest should be applied only with pen and applied first to the space-defining surfaces, beginning with the floor or ground plane. These surfaces should always be rendered continuously because intermittent texturing destroys the perception of the surface as a continuous background. Objects standing in front of these textured surfaces should never be textured; rather, they should remain open silhouettes so the viewer's perception continues past them to the textured surface beyond. The choice of how to render textures is always a critical decision and should be based on the most difficult place you will have to draw the texture. If the material is limited in area and in the foreground, like the floor tile in the perspective at right, you can draw it with a double-line joint with great effect and without spending a great deal of time. If the same tile had been extended outside on the walk leading to the distant building, such an indication wouldn't work. It would have been physically impossible to draw it beyond the doorway.

The indication of materials in a design drawing is crucial to an understanding of what the environment will be like when built. Textural interest is the most intimate of the interest categories because it cues remembered tactile experiences. The drawing of a brick floor triggers our remembrance of what it feels like to walk barefoot across a cool brick floor on a hot summer day.

Being able to draw a broad range of materials is important for a designer because as long as we make our own design drawings, we probably won't work with materials we can't draw successfully. Therefore, we need to draw them all, or at least the ones we prefer.

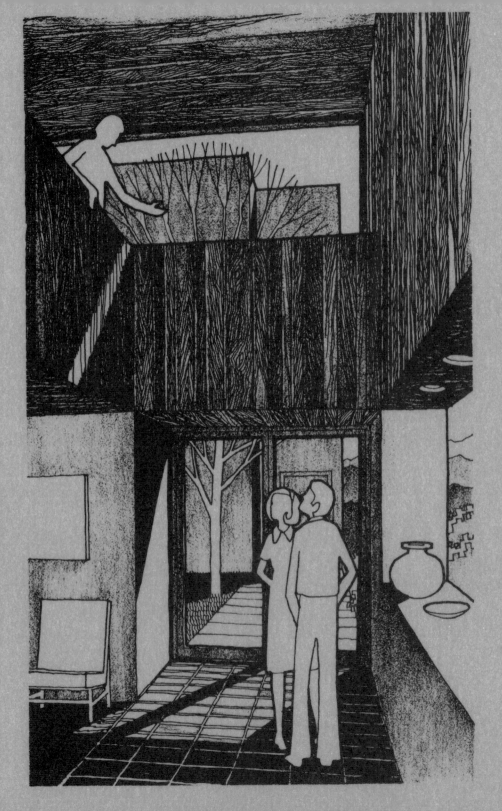

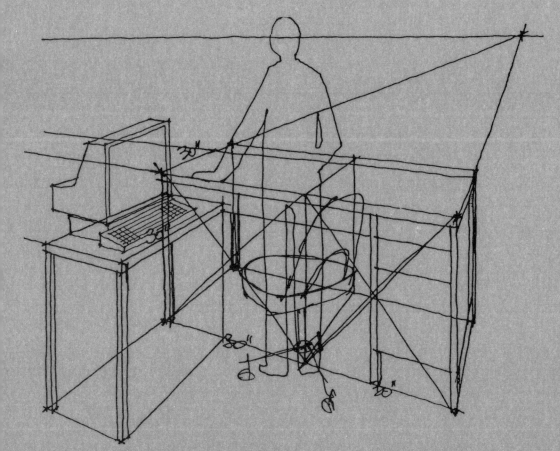

OVERLAID REFINEMENT

The following experiences are designed to help students develop the ability to refine a crude sketch into a series of more resolved drawings by overlaying the first rough sketches with successive layers of tracing paper. Tracing paper is a marvelous, underappreciated invention. It allows you to have a second, third, or fourth shot and compare proposed changes with the previous underlay.

Designers should learn to visualize design drawing not as a single drawing, but as a potential stack of drawings progressing from a very crude sketch at the bottom to a very slick, detailed rendering at the top. When you have the disciplined ability to raise any rough sketch through these various levels, drawing becomes a matter of free choice, depending on the purpose of the drawing and the time available.

It takes a while to develop the skill and confidence to refine a rough sketch and know where you're going with it, and it's always tempting to try to make a drawing halfway up the stack without completing the supporting underlays. The drawing and placement of figures, trees, furniture, and shadows always need the benefit of overlaid refinement.

OVERLAID REFINEMENT

The following experiences are designed to help students develop the ability to refine a crude sketch into a series of more resolved drawings by overlaying the first rough sketches with successive layers of tracing paper. Tracing paper is a marvelous, underappreciated invention. It allows you to have a second, third, or fourth shot and compare proposed changes with the previous underlay.

Designers should learn to visualize design drawing not as a single drawing, but as a potential stack of drawings progressing from a very crude sketch at the bottom to a very slick, detailed rendering at the top. When you have the disciplined ability to raise any rough sketch through these various levels, drawing becomes a matter of free choice, depending on the purpose of the drawing and the time available.

It takes a while to develop the skill and confidence to refine a rough sketch and know where you're going with it, and it's always tempting to try to make a drawing halfway up the stack without completing the supporting underlays. The drawing and placement of figures, trees, furniture, and shadows always need the benefit of overlaid refinement.

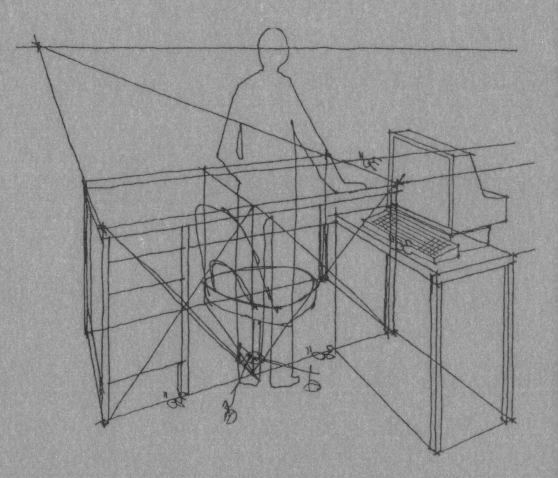

These drawings reflect the first and second overlays of the base drawing on page 119. They are examples of the kind of overlay you will be asked to make in the next exercises. The notes below indicate the kind of self-critical evaluation designers should always make of their drawings. Continued self-evaluation is one of the best habits you can form.

The desk and the chair are now okay. The figures need more refinement and the telephone cord needs help. The woman's hair and ankle are awkward and the keys on the computer keyboard are redundant, and it is probably impossible to draw them well at this scale.

Not bad, but the woman's hand was better in the previous sketch, and the human situation seems a little male chauvinistic. The woman's hair texture is also probably too much—it conflicts with the wood grain.

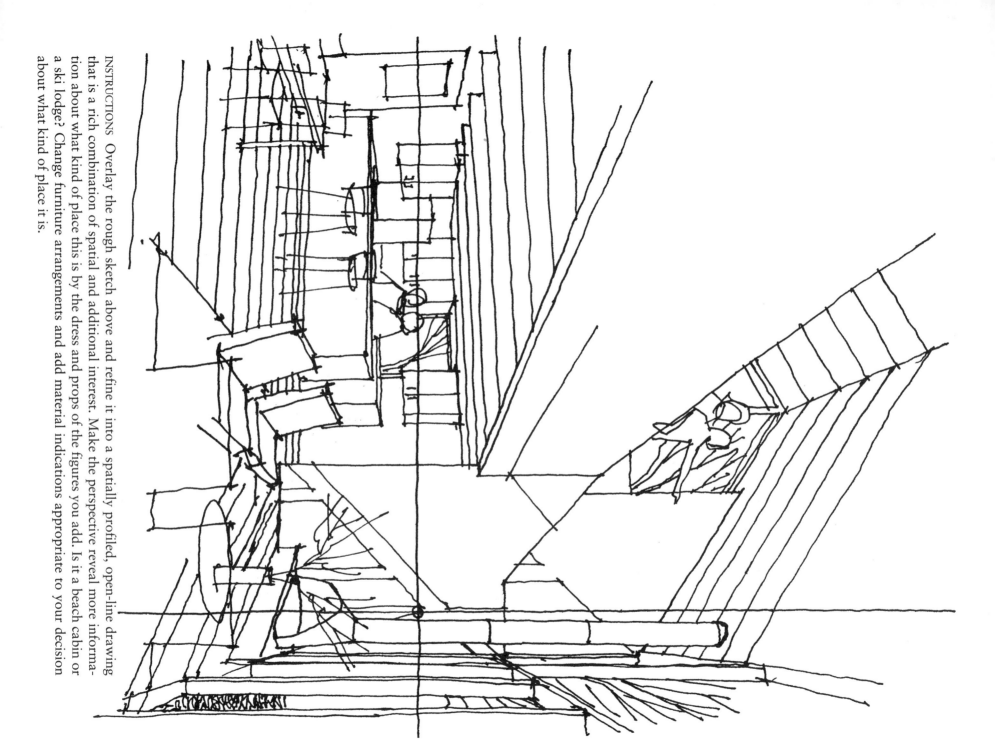

INSTRUCTIONS Overlay the rough sketch above and refine it into a spatially profiled, open-line drawing that is a rich combination of spatial and additional interest. Make the perspective reveal more information about what kind of place this is by the dress and props of the figures you add. Is it a beach cabin or a ski lodge? Change furniture arrangements and add material indications appropriate to your decision about what kind of place it is.

INSTRUCTIONS Overlay the rough sketch above and refine it into a spatially profiled, open-line drawing that is a rich combination of spatial and additional interest. Make the perspective reveal more information about what kind of place it represents by adding windows and doors and by specifying materials, signs, and dress and props for the figures. The space could look like an office complex, a shopping center, or a university.

INSTRUCTIONS Overlay the rough sketch above and refine it into a spatially profiled, open-line drawing that is a rich combination of spatial and additional interest. Make the perspective reveal more information about what kind of place it represents by adding windows and doors and by specifying materials, signs, and dress and props for the figures. Depending on what you add, the space could look like an office complex, a hotel, or an urban university.

124

INSTRUCTIONS Overlay the rough sketch above and refine it into a spatially profiled, open-line drawing that is a rich combination of spatial and additional interest. Make the perspective reveal more information about what kind of place it represents by adding signs and dress and props for the figures. Depending on your changes and additions, it could look like a reception room for a pediatrician's office, an attorney's office, or a travel agency.

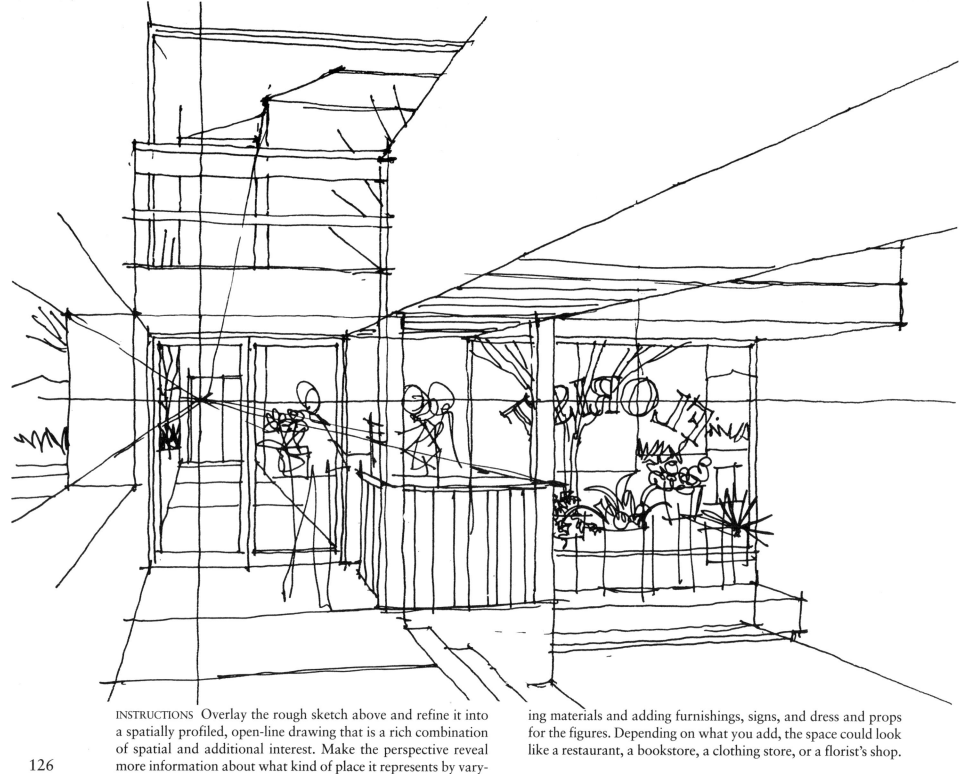

INSTRUCTIONS Overlay the rough sketch above and refine it into a spatially profiled, open-line drawing that is a rich combination of spatial and additional interest. Make the perspective reveal more information about what kind of place it represents by vary-ing materials and adding furnishings, signs, and dress and props for the figures. Depending on what you add, the space could look like a restaurant, a bookstore, a clothing store, or a florist's shop.

INSTRUCTIONS Overlay the rough sketch above and refine it into a spatially profiled, open-line drawing that is a rich combination of spatial and additional interest. Make the perspective indicate choices that are only suggested in the sketch. What should the paving and wall materials be? Should the seating be fixed or movable? Will the fountain work where it is indicated? Is the landscaping adequate or should there be more? Is there a place for an outdoor sculpture?

127

REPRODUCTION TECHNIQUES

These experiences are designed to help students learn the options offered by today's technology in the reproduction of drawings. Some reproduction techniques are great time-savers while others can help you produce very slick, professional-looking renderings. All offer the great advantage of preserving the original drawing for future modification or further reproduction.

The greatest time-saving technique reproductions offer is the production of middletone drawings, the most dramatic being night perspectives. The simplest way to produce a middletone drawing is to make a mylar or photocopy print of your original drawing on tracing paper and mount the print on a very dark board. This will immediately turn your drawing into a middletone drawing, and white Prismacolor™ or white paper cutouts can be added to the underside of the translucent print.

This technique also works beautifully for plans and sections. White paper cutouts under the interior, enclosed space of the plan or section give the drawings a powerful tonal interest that would have taken hours to complete by toning the white paper surrounding the plan or section gray.

Another way to obtain a good middletone drawing from an ink-line drawing is simply to have a quality photocopy run on middletone paper. This wasn't possible before the invention of the photocopy machine, when such a drawing could only be produced very laboriously by smudging the back of the original drawing or print with graphite and then trace-transferring the drawing carbon-paper style.

Perhaps the most popular reproduction technique used in making presentation drawings is still Diazo process prints on various papers (sepia, brownline, blueline, blackline, or mylar) at various speeds, with Prismacolor™ or felt-tip markers applied to the resulting print. The reason this standard "blueprinting" (as it is mistakenly called) process is used so much is because nearly every architect's, landscape architect's, and interior designer's office has a Diazo printer, and the convenience and control of running your own prints is hard to beat.

Underexposure of the various papers, especially sepia and brownline, produces a beautiful brown tone, even when the original drawing was untouched white. Usually this print tone is assumed to be the value of shade, with shadows rendered darker before the print is made. The subsequent addition of light tones, sunlit surfaces, sky, and sky reflections in glass makes a very dramatic rendering.

Another popular use of reproduction techniques is the cut-and-paste photocopy technique. This is a very effective way of pasting cutout entourage (figures, trees, furniture, automobiles) into your drawing. Once the cutting and pasting is finished you can run large photocopies on tracing paper and still have all the options described above open to you.

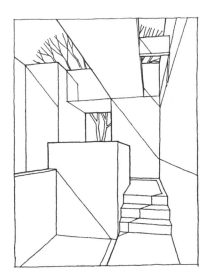

INSTRUCTIONS Get a very dark brownline or sepia print of this drawing and make it into a night perspective by coloring illuminated interior surfaces (seen through the windows) and exterior sidewalks and soffits with cream or sand Prismacolor™ pencils.

Also, illuminate the exterior sidewalls and soffits at right, even though we can't see the glass directly. You may also want to add a few stars and illumination on the steps from hidden step lights.

129

INSTRUCTIONS Get a very dark brownline or sepia print of this drawing and make it into a night perspective by coloring illuminated interior surfaces (seen through the windows) and exterior sidewalks and soffits with cream or sand Prismacolor™ pencils.

Also, illuminate the exterior sidewalks and soffits at right, even though we can't see the glass directly. You may also want to add a few stars and illumination on the steps from hidden step lights.

INSTRUCTIONS For a daytime rendering, shadows and glass reflections are added. Make a medium brownline or sepia print and color by adding a nonphoto-blue Prismacolor™ sky and sky reflections in the glass, white on the sunlit walls, brown to the wood, brick red on the paving and roofs, and various greens to the landscaping.

INSTRUCTIONS: For a daytime rendering, shadows and glass reflections are added. Make a medium brownline or sepia print and color by adding a nonphoto-blue Prismacolor™ sky and sky reflections in the glass, white on the sunlit walls, brown to the wood, brick red on the paving and roofs, and various greens to the landscaping.

INSTRUCTIONS Turn this drawing over and apply white Prisma-color™ to the back of the glass areas of the big window wall facing us. Turn this over and place on carefully selected dark paper.

Quickly color (consistent with the sketch quality) the front of the drawing, using light colors for sunlit surfaces. Apply the color at the same stroking angle as the sketch.

133

INSTRUCTIONS: Turn this drawing over and apply white Prisma-color™ to the back of the glass areas of the big window wall facing us. Turn this over and place on carefully selected dark paper.

Quickly color (consistent with the sketch quality) the front of the drawing, using light colors for sunlit surfaces. Apply the color at the same stroking angle as the sketch.

INSTRUCTIONS Get a mylar print (matte back or wrong-reading on the emulsion). Try mounting the mylar on a brown board—you may not need to color the wood! Apply Prismacolor™ pencil to the matte back of the mylar, beginning by coloring the sky and its reflec-tions in the glass, then coloring the mountains. Continue working your way forward, coloring the foreground, the figures, and the tree trunks last, if at all.

135

INSTRUCTIONS Get a mylar print (matte back or wrong-reading on the emulsion). Try mounting the mylar on a brown board—you may not need to color the wood! Apply Prismacolor™ pencil to the matte back of the mylar, beginning by coloring the sky and its reflec-

tions in the glass, then coloring the mountains. Continue working your way forward, coloring the foreground, the figures, and the tree trunks last, if at all.

BLACK-AND-WHITE ON MIDDLETONE

The middletone pages that follow are duplicates of previous experiences. They allow you to try making black-and-white-on-middletone drawings. Until recently this technique demanded the tedious step of transferring a tracing-paper original drawing onto opaque middletone paper. Now, however, there are photocopy machines that can, from a tracing paper sketch, produce a high-quality copy on a middletone paper of your choice. You will want to choose your papers carefully at an art store because the colors stocked by most photocopy shops are pastels that won't help you make good-looking renderings.

If you have a white pencil handy take a few minutes and try adding white to the sunlit surfaces of the drawings at left. The whitest surfaces should be the upward-facing horizontal surfaces; next whitest the vertical surfaces facing us; and least white the vertical surfaces facing toward the left.

Nothing compares with this technique's rendering of light. It is always a pleasure for me to see how the sunlit surfaces seem to jump up off the middletone paper when you hit them with the white pencil. If you have the basic drawing, it takes just minutes to produce a really dramatic sketch—and, somehow, you get all the credit for the middletone paper you didn't even have to touch.

INSTRUCTIONS This experience is meant to demonstrate how quickly you can add color to a photocopy on middletone paper. The trick is to add only colors that are lighter than the paper, assuming you added the shades and shadows before you got the photocopy. This means, generally, that you should color only the sky and the sunlit surfaces, with just a light tinting of landscaping and other surfaces. Apply the color quickly to match the sketch.

139

INSTRUCTIONS This drawing is meant to be colored more carefully than that on page 139. As with the drawing on page 133, begin by coloring the exterior space, seen through the window wall, much lighter than the interior space. Then color the interior surfaces. The sunlit surfaces should be subdued and not as bright as the exterior. Be aware that the lines of a photocopy, unlike this offset-printed page, are just toner and may be displaced by careless coloring.

INSTRUCTIONS This drawing lets you experience the dilemma of whether to laboriously color between the lines or just apply a very light coating of color over the lines so that they still show clearly. The sky, sky reflections, steps, planter, and foundation wall at left are no problem. The foreground paving might even be colored between the lines, but wood and all surfaces in shade or shadow should be just lightly washed with color so lines are not obscured.